Fight for the Falklands!

Fight for the Falklands!
JOHN LAFFIN

St. Martin's Press
New York

Library of Congress Catalog Card Number 82-61226
ISBN 0-312-28868-9

First published in Great Britain in 1982 by Sphere Books Limited.

First U.S. Edition
10 9 8 7 6 5 4 3 2 1

*To the other warriors —
the war correspondents*

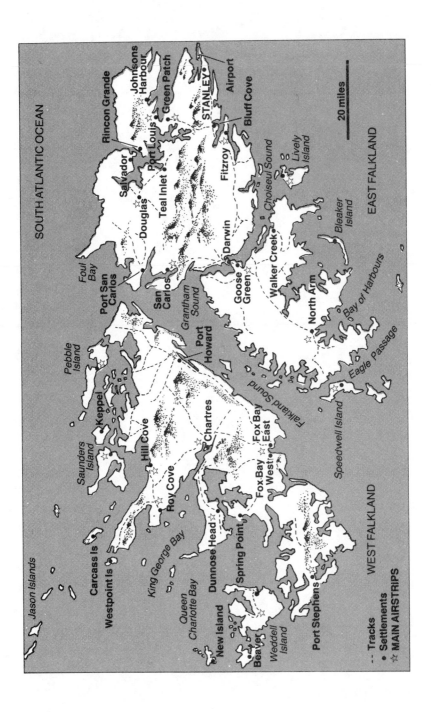

Fight for the Falklands!

1 Invasion

Falkland Islanders, the frontier people of the far South Atlantic, made hardy by the harsh climate of their storm-swept islands, always get up early. On the morning of Friday 2 April 1982 the 1,060 people of the capital, Port Stanley, were brought to their feet specially early – by the sound of gunfire.

The Kelpers – as they call themselves from the masses of seaweed in the surrounding oceans – were being wrenched from geographical and historical isolation by an invasion that had been feared, intermittently, for 149 years. The first war noises came from Argentinian commandos who hit the beach under cover of darkness and secured the small airport, six miles from the capital. At dawn the startled and frightened Falklanders peering from behind cover saw what seemed to be a large army pouring in on landing craft. In fact there were 2,500 men in all, backed by an aircraft carrier, the British-built *Vienticinco de Mayo* (25th May), three missile-carrying destroyers and other warships.

Opposing them, as a garrison for the whole of the Falkland Islands, an area the size of Wales, as well as the Dependency of South Georgia, 800 miles away, were just eighty-four Royal Marines.

It seemed obvious from the beginning that the Argentinians were shooting to kill; at Government

House bullets were hitting the wooden walls at waist height as the Governor, Rex Hunt, his wife Mavis and his son and daughter lay flat on the floor. A hand grenade exploded in the kitchen and water poured from punctured pipes. Other homes also suffered damage.

The tough and disciplined Marines, though surprised in their sleep by the invasion, fought back for three hours, killing perhaps fifteen enemy and wounding seventeen without loss to themselves. Hunt just had time to get off a radio message to London before an Argentinian officer was asking him to surrender, as 'a reasonable man'. Hunt, aged fifty-five, and as as cool as a former Spitfire pilot would be, demanded that the officer should himself come to Government House carrying a white flag. It was a characteristic British gesture, in hopeless circum-stances, to make the enemy appear to be surrendering. But Hunt was under no illusions; fearing a massacre he ordered the marines through their commander, Major Gary Noott, to lay down their arms.

They did so reluctantly and one small group headed for the country to resist from there. Cold, hungry and wet they arrived at the Watsons' farm at Long Island settlement where they dried their clothes and were fed. When an Argentine helicopter arrived to pick them up, only their fears for the farming family persuaded them to surrender.

Hunt refused to shake hands with the Argentinian General, who told him that he was being 'very ungentlemanly'. Hunt, a stocky man who can be pugnacious when he wishes, replied angrily, 'I think it very uncivilised to invade British territory. You are here illegally.' The Argentinians were not inclined to engage in a debate. Two days later Hunt was told he was leaving the Falklands with just what he could carry. Defiant in the only way he could be he donned his ceremonial uniform and plumed hat and his chauffeur drove him to the Port Stanley airport in his official limousine, an Austin of London taxi-cab type. A small Union flag fluttered defiantly from the hood and the escorting Argentinians allowed it to remain. Hunt and his family were flown to Uruguay, en route to their homeland.

Next day, 3 April, another Argentinian invasion force appeared at Grytviken, South Georgia, where Lieutenant Keith Mills commanded twenty-two Royal Marines. In a seven-hour battle his tiny force killed three Argentinian soldiers, crippled a helicopter and damaged a corvette before being over-whelmed. None of the Marines was seriously hurt. Lieutenant Mills was later awarded the Distinguished Service Cross for his courage and leadership.

Ignominiously, the former defenders were bundled out of the Falklands to Uruguay, from where they travelled to London. The Falklands became the Malvinas and the islanders became an occupied people under a military governor, General Mario Benjamin Menendez. The Argentinians set about the task of massively reinforcing the invasion force.

They had humiliated a once-great power and had precipitated one of the most extraordinary wars of the century. The events which were to flow from the invasion affected, in one way or another, virtually every country in the world; they fanned a fiery nationalism in the aggressor country and they awakened the warrior spirit of their British victims, a people who had thought that this spirit had died with the end of their empire.

The conflict aroused passions and prejudices, created alliances and enmities, alarmed the super-powers, built some reputations and destroyed others and changed many perceptions about the purpose and practice of war. In media interest the Falklands War eclipsed even the Vietnam War at its most dramatic and controversial and became part of the war itself. *Time* Magazine, on 10 May, saw the conflict as 'the oddity it has been since the beginning – a case of nineteenth century gunboat confrontation in the late twentieth century'. It would not remain at the oddity level for very long. Soon it would become the first missile war.

Above all, on 2 April 1982, the Argentinians shocked the peace-loving world community into a new awareness of its own vulnerability. And not only to the dangers of maverick military action. It became clear that even among normally civilised people the emotions of anger and revenge, pride and patriotism can quickly become irrational and therefore dangerous.

2 The Intelligence Failure

The roots of the Falkland crisis are historic (see Appendix) but in the previous ten years, right until the day of the invasion, it had been building up because of an Intelligence failure, by both the British and the Argentinians. Military and political Intelligence – or the lack of attention paid to it – was lamentable. Neither side understood the nature of the other.

The 'modern period' of the Britain-Argentine dispute can be dated from 1965 when the U.N. General Assembly asked the British and Argentinians to hold talks with a view to finding a 'peaceful solution' to their respective claims about sovereignty. Meetings took place nearly every year and by 1971 the Argentinians had additional incentive in their drive for sovereignty. A report, which was attributed to a Shell survey and to computer findings, speculated that there was enough oil between the Falklands and the Patagonian coast to justify the label of 'New Kuwait'. Shell warned that the report was 'merely an unsubstantiated estimate' but it caused excitement in Buenos Aires when leaked by the Argentine army chief-of-staff.

The 1972 meeting led to an agreement by the Argentinians to establish sea and air links and postal services and, in Buenos Aires, educational and

5

medical facilities for Falkland Islanders. The Government also licensed the state oil company to provide fuel for the Falklands. As the British objected to none of this the Argentinians took it as a sign that the British were ready to 'let go' the Falklands.

In 1976 the Argentine illegally established a scientific research station on South Thule, an island in the South Sandwich group, a part of the Falklands Islands Dependency, 900 miles to the east. The authorities went to bizarre lengths to arrange for the wife of one of the scientists on South Thule to give birth there to manufacture a claim that the place must now be regarded as Argentinian territory. The British made several protests about the presence on Thule, all of which were ignored, and the base was still there in 1982. To the Argentinians this was another encouraging sign.

After some tension in 1976 both countries withdrew their ambassadors and that same year an Argentine destroyer fired a shot over the bows of a British ship in disputed waters. The dispute lapsed and ties were re-established in 1980. The incident was too quickly forgotten in Whitehall.

Some potentially difficult situations were discreetly overcome. In 1977, for instance, the British Labour Government of James Callaghan, hearing about Argentinian plans for an 'invasion', assembled some warships and stood them about 400 miles off the Falklands. The Argentinians, not wanting serious trouble, took the hint.

But later a British economic survey mentioned the need for closer links with Argentina. Britain then quietly announced that perhaps the time had indeed come to consider a new framework of political and economic co-operation. The Argentinians read this as evidence that Britain was not seriously interested in retaining the Falklands. One of their Intelligence documents reported that 'Great Britain is in a desperate economic situation and would like to be able to cut off the Malvinas (the Argentinian name for the islands). If we occupy the islands without violence the British will make a great noise but will do nothing. They will be glad to get rid of one more colony, especially when all their military strength is committed to NATO and Northern Ireland.' The Argentinian Intelligence analysts also noted that the British had never said 'No' over the Malvinas while they often said 'Perhaps' and 'In time'. In this the British were culpable; in effect they allowed the Argentinian leaders to believe they could, under certain circumstances, obtain the islands.

But one event more than any other was taken by the Argentinians to mean that Britain was tired of the liability of the Falklands. In 1980 Nicholas Ridley, a Foreign Office Minister, visited the Falklands and strongly suggested a compromise involving the ceding of titular sovereignty to Argentina in return for full British rights for a certain period – the 'Hong Kong arrangement'. The islanders rejected the idea but Buenos Aires marked down Ridley's suggestion.

True, successive British governments had said that nothing could be done without the Falkland Islanders' consent but the Argentinian military caste did not take this seriously. A mere 1,800 people, most of them mere sheepfarmers, were insignificant and would do what London told them. The Argentinian dictatorship, ruthless against opposition, had had much experience in getting its own people to do what they were told; at least 15,000 who had not known what was good for them had 'disappeared'.

The Argentinian Foreign Ministry was badly informed by its embassy in London. It reported in February 1982 that the British were militarily weak and that its navy was 'virtually non-existent'. Yet at that very moment twenty-eight Navy vessels were being built and some of them were due for sea trials within weeks. A major Argentinian mistake was in its London Embassy's assessment of the British people. 'The English (sic) public will not fight for the Malvinas. The English will never again go to war for a colony. After the Suez defeat they gave up the rest of their empire and the Labour Ministry [it was a Conservative Ministry when the report was written] refuses to have modern weapons. The English will not go to war again except to defend England directly.'

On the basis of all this it must have seemed to the Junta and the thirty to forty other men who held great power in Argentina that invasion of the Falklands had a good chance of being 'accepted' by the British. Would they really fight for 1,800 people, 600,000 sheep and 200 mostly uninhabited wind-swept islands 8,000 miles from Britain. No, they would not. Indeed, they had neither the money nor the means.

The British decision to withdraw H.M.S. *Endurance* from the South Atlantic – and not to replace it – was also seen by the Argentinians as yet further evidence that the British were withdrawing. On 30 March the Labour peer, Lord Shackleton, told the House of Lords that a friend at the Argentine Embassy had asked him a few months before to confirm that the permanent recall of H.M.S. *Endurance* meant that the British were on the way out. 'I of course denied this vigorously,' Lord Shackleton said. But the Argentinians have long been accustomed to vigorous British denials – accompanied by what they took to be lack of political will. In his own lengthy report on the Falklands, Lord Shackleton referred to them as 'islands surrounded by a sea of advice' – reference to the many surveys of the Falklands' future.

From the other direction, British political and military intelligence sent to London from Argentina appears to have been fairly complete, but because it seemed merely to repeat information given many times before it was not considered seriously enough at the Foreign Office and at the Ministry of Defence. In any case the Falklands were not a Foreign Office priority. It had long been preoccupied with improving and consolidating Britain's relations with other members of the EEC and with encouraging the Palestine Liberation Organisation. It failed to foresee the Portuguese revolution and the downfall of the Shah of Iran.

Four Foreign Office staff in particular would be able to answer the difficult questions about Britain's lack of preparedness at the time of the Argentinian invasion. They were the head of the F.O., Sir Michael Palliser, and the three officials responsible for advising Lord Carrington and his junior ministers.

They were the head of the South American department, Patrick Fearn, an assistant secretary, Mr Bright, and Alex Smith, of the 'Falklands desk' itself.

While the Argentinians were misreading the British, the British – or more precisely the permanent staff at the Foreign Office – were making miscalculations about the Argentinians. They considered that the Argentinians, as emotional Latin people, were incapable of incisive action. After all, they had been in a state of agitation about the Falklands for a century and more and would probably continue in that state for another hundred years. In any case, with the highest inflation rate in the world at 148 per cent and fierce internal dissent, the leaders had enough to worry about without 'going military' over the Falklands. The fallacy of this argument, which was actually presented during a discussion in the Foreign Office, was that precisely because of the staggering inflation and the problems it was causing the leadership needed a diversion. Another psychological miscalculation was that General Leopoldo Fortunato Galtieri, the leader of the three-man military Junta, was not the type of man to go into action across an ocean. This may have been true of Galtieri, who had assumed power in December 1981, but it did not apply to Admiral Jorge Issac Anaya, 55, and Air Force Brigadier General Arturo Lami Dozo, 53. The Junta operated on a consensus basis which usually went Anaya's way, as he is the most hawkish. At one time Anaya moved Argentina's only aircraft carrier, *Vienticinco de Mayo*, out to sea without even telling Galtieri. This was in itself worthy of Intelligence comment. From as early as 24 February the British press had been warning of suspicious Argentinian movements.

Another warning sign apparently not adequately heeded was a long article in the leading Buenos Aires newspaper, *La Prensa*, late in January; this article told how General Galtieri had promised to possess the Malvinas islands before 3 January 1983, before the British and the Falklanders could celebrate the 150th anniversary of British settlement. This promise, or threat, was well known in Buenos Aires and while in itself it could be seen as a dictator's rhetoric in combination with other pointers it was a warning of imminent action.

About a month before the invasion Argentina asked the Defence Ministry if it could buy the delta-wing Vulcans, which were to be phased out of the R.A.F. by the end of 1982 and replaced by Tornado swing-wing aircraft. Possession of the Vulcans would have made Argentina the only South American nation to own a strategic bomber force. In a war with Britain it could have dropped conventional bombs on the Falklands, South Georgia and even, with in-flight refuelling, on Ascension Island. The Ministry did not follow up the offer but there is no evidence to show that it reported the matter to the Foreign Office.

Now the unpredictable, often an element in international relations, came into play through the person of Señor Constantino Davidoff, aged 40, a wealthy scrap metal dealer from Buenos Aires. In 1976 Davidoff had heard about three whaling stations on the South Georgia Islands which had been abandoned in 1964. Much scrap metal was

11

involved and Davidoff foresaw a good profit. In September 1979 he signed a contract with the stations' owner, Christian Salveson of Edinburgh and in December 1981 he made a short trip to South Georgia, with British permission, to inspect the islands. Davidoff, as requested, later sent the Embassy the names of the men who would be going to South Georgia to work on the old factories; he has an Embassy receipt for this list.

The forty or so workers arrived at Leith on 19 March, aboard the *Bahia Buen Susesco*, said by the British to be a naval vessel. Whether or not the Davidoff men were supposed to report officially to the leader of the British Arctic Survey team at Grytviken, on the other side of the bay, is disputed. But it is clear that they shot a deer, feasted themselves and as a patriotic prank raised a blue-and-white Argentinian flag over their salvage operation. Some of the British rowed across to the Argentinians to object to the flag and to tell the Argentinians that they were illegal immigrants. The situation was not particularly tense and some of the Englishmen accepted roast venison. The Argentinians hauled down the flag promptly enough and all but about ten of them left in the *Bahia Buen Susesco*.

The scientists may now have over-reacted, for they sent a radio message which said – or more likely was interpreted as saying – that there had been an 'Argentine landing'. The message was picked up in Port Stanley and again there was over-reaction. A group of islanders briefly occupied the office of the Argentine airline; one scrawled 'UK – OK' on an outside wall, another used toothpaste to write on a mirror 'Tit for tat'. It is a fair assumption that the airline staff were mystified about this action.

The Foreign Office, on 22 March, protested to the Argentine Government that the Davidoff crew had landed illegally; unless the official Embassy seals on Davidoff's documents are a forgery, this was not so. Two days later, on 24 March, H.M.S. *Endurance* – an outdated irrelevance as a warship and itself destined to become scrap metal under navy pruning plans – was sent to keep an eye on the scrap metal merchants and to land a small party of Royal Marines.

In turn Argentina despatched a warship to 'protect' the men at Leith. It was probably at this point that the Junta saw their opportunity, for another five warships were quickly ordered into the area, a clear case of irrational overkill or rational scheming. Britain meanwhile sent another ship, the *John Biscoe* and more Marines.

On 30 March Lord Carrington, the Foreign Secretary, who had hurriedly returned from a trip to the Middle East, announced to Parliament that a 'potentially dangerous situation' existed. He was referring to Argentina's claim that while the Davidoff men had adequate documents they did not need them; the South Georgia islands were a dependency of the Falklands, so the scrap metal men were on Argentine soil.

But the key word was *potentially*. The most obvious indication that Argentina could not engage in military adventures abroad was – as the British Embassy in Buenos Aires and the Foreign Office in London saw it – the massive internal unrest. Only two days before the Falklands invasion, the trade unions organised a street demonstration; a crowd tried to march on the city Central Plaza and they called for an end to military rule and economic mismanagement. They fought a bloody battle with troops and police who shot and wounded six demonstrators and roughly arrested 2,000 others. It was the worst unrest since 1976.

Then came the invasion. It swept aside all social unrest and in a burst of national pride the Argentinians united themselves behind the Junta against the British. In the wave of emotional euphoria the government released all the 2,000 political protesters it had just thrown into gaol. An imprisoned union leader, who might well have been fearing that he would be murdered, was invited to attend the swearing in of the military governor of the Malvinas, the newly proclaimed twenty-third province of Argentina.

One man who deserved to be asked was Constantino Davidoff, though he was not really interested in politics. Son of a Bulgarian father and a Greek mother, he has a purely mercantile mind. Six weeks into the war he told a *Guardian* reporter, 'If I had never been born Argentina and Great Britain would not be fighting'. More thoughtful and informed Argentinians, such as journalists, would know that Davidoff was assuming too much blame; they knew that the Junta had manipulated the crisis – and if this one had not occurred they would have found another. The journalists knew too that Argentina would be politically and economically isolated but they joined in the ecstatic celebrations and street parades with brass bands and showers of flowers. Nobody, it seemed, cared where the dramatic first step taken by Galtieri, Anaya and Dozo might lead them.

Argentina was, in fact, behaving as it might reasonably be expected to by anybody with just a little knowledge of Latin American politics and history.

Britain had also behaved in a predictable way. This was why it had made the costliest foreign and defence policy miscalculation in twenty-five years and why less than one hundred Royal Marines could not hold one of the last thirteen outposts of Empire against waves of jubilant Argentinian troops.

3 Test of Nerves

In their decision to invade the Falkland Islands the Argentinian leaders made a major sexist miscalculation. They under-estimated Margaret Thatcher.

This error of judgment is understandable, because Argentinian men, from the president down to the schoolboy, are victims of machismo. V. S. Naipaul, the distinguished novelist, who has studied Argentinian society, says, 'There is the machismo of the football field or the racing track. And there is machismo as simple stylishness. The police motor cyclist, for instance, goggled and gloved, weaving about at speed, siren going, clearing a path for an official car. But machismo is really about the conquest and humiliation of women. In the sterile society it is the victimisation by the simple of the simpler ...'

Argentinian women have few rights; most accept that they are being reared for early marriage or for domestic service. In contrast, all males have macho and for all of them sexual conquest is a duty. As Naipaul says, sex has little to do with passion or even attraction. Argentina has an enormous brothel industry, great buildings with neon signs; right in the middle of Buenos Aires is an avenue of apartmented brothels.

The one great exception to the subjugation of

16

women was Isabel Peron – made an exception by the great name she bore. Indeed, she was an aberration in Argentinian politics, she died demented, and the Galtieri-Anaya-Dozo Junta are glad there is no longer an Isabel Peron.

From the time that Mrs Thatcher became Prime Minister of the United Kingdom in May 1979 the expansionists among the military caste in Argentina began to suspect, in their obsession about the Falklands, that their time had come. They watched carefully to see just how much authority this woman could maintain. It was obvious that she had become leader of her party because men had elected her, but the Argentinian generals assumed that she was the result of a compromise made by strong men with equal following. Therefore, she would be dominated by the men who had put her into the leadership.

The Galtieri Junta reasoned that no woman would want war; further, no woman could politically direct a war. Accustomed to facing down and conquering women in their own society, the Argentinian leaders really believed that Mrs Thatcher was the weak link of the British government. When the Falklands were invaded and she at once assumed an almost Churchillian command of her nation's resources practically all Argentinians were startled. Even the women, who might have been expected to applaud a woman standing up to men, resented Mrs Thatcher, probably because she was able to do what none of them had been able to do.

In Buenos Aires, the grotesque and often crude magazine covers and posters, with their accompanying abusive epithets, were as much a reflection of

Argentinian frustration as of dislike for Mrs Thatcher as leader of an enemy nation.

The Argentinian military leaders were also ignorant of the type of tradition under which Mrs Thatcher was educated: the principle that Britain protects and defends its own people, at almost any cost and anywhere in the world. I gave an educated Argentinian a list of the places to which British governments over the last century have sent expeditions to protect British subjects or to punish those who had attacked them. They include China, Tibet, Afghanistan, various parts of India, Burma, Iraq, Iran, a score of countries in east, central, west and south Africa, Egypt, the Sudan, and the Malay archipelago. I think he did not believe me. 'Tibet!' he said. 'Why would the British send an army to Tibet of all places?'

When I told him it was to rescue a trade mission attacked by the Tibetans, in 1903–4, I think he disbelieved me – until I showed him the medal awarded to the soldiers who had fought in the campaign.

In her instant and unquestioning decision to go to the Falkland Islands 'of all places', Mrs Thatcher not only followed a British tradition but showed that she was indeed the nation's leader and the party chief, when the occupation of the Falklands became known in London. She was also at once aware that someone in a high place had blundered or had been negligent for Britain to have been caught so completely off guard. In this crisis Parliament was recalled for an emergency session on Saturday 3 April, the first such weekend sitting of parliament since the Suez Crisis of 1956.

The historic proceedings were compared in emotional intensity with the debate over the defeat of a British force sent to Norway which brought down Neville Chamberlain in 1940. Mrs Thatcher was not brought down but the debate was exciting enough. The Government was defensive and the performance of its speakers was inept. For instance, while claiming Opposition support in a national emergency, Defence Secretary Nott sneeringly referred to 'the new Labour Party' – the s.d.p. Deputy-Foreign Secretary Humphrey Atkins did not inspire confidence by explaining that when he said he had heard from the Governor, Rex Hunt, at 10.30 a.m. on Friday morning, he had meant 8.30 a.m.

All parties certainly shared the same anxiety and anger, perhaps even the same ideas about retaliation. It was just that they expressed themselves differently. Julian Amery wanted war, if necessary, 'to wipe the stain off Britain's honour'. Sir Peter Emery also wanted war – if the outcome could be ninety-nine per cent certain. Edward du Cann invoked the memory of the Duke of Wellington. David Owen, speaking from the strength of a former Foreign Secretary who had scared off the Argentinians in 1977, also thought that war might be necessary. The most bellicose speaker from the Labour benches was Michael Foot, who made it clear that he expected the Prime Minister to carry out her pledge to free the Falklands from fascist rule. She would only escape the charge of betraying them by her deeds. He created the belief, throughout the House, that he was calling for war and a Conservative congratulated him on 'speaking for England'.

The former Prime Minister, James Callaghan, in a statesman-like speech, was clearly appealing for parliamentary unity in the face of the Argentinians' naked aggression. Callaghan's former Foreign Secretary, David Owen, told Mr Nott that if he could not see the advantage of negotiating from military strength he should not be Defence Secretary.

Enoch Powell made an eloquent speech in which he suggested, unfairly, that some of the Royal Marines who had garrisoned the islands should be courtmartialled for not fighting long or hard enough. But his most memorable observation was that it would not be long before everybody knew what type of metal the Iron Lady was really made of.

Much criticised in Parliament, by the press and public, Lord Carrington stressed that he was not guilty of failing to foresee Galtieri's intentions. But somebody in the Foreign Office was guilty and convention demanded that the Secretary resign.

It is worth quoting here from a speech made by Lord Carrington on 25 March to the Royal Institute of International Affairs, which was also broadcast by the B.B.C. During this lecture he said: 'The real role of the Foreign Secretary is to define this country's overseas interests; to choose between those that may conflict; to decide on the methods needed to further the major interests; and then to see that those decisions are carried out ... My decisions, if they are to be sensible ones, need to be based on the right information and on expert advice ... Britain's power to impose her will beyond her own shores has diminished to the point where it can rarely if ever be a substitute for diplomacy ... The job of British Foreign Secretary is as exhilarating as ever ...'

It would have been difficult for Lord Carrington not to resign after this but Mrs Thatcher and the Deputy-Prime Minister, William Whitelaw, suggested a face-saving ploy: the Foreign Secretary would offer his resignation, Mrs Thatcher would refuse to accept it and he would then withdraw his offer. In this way he would have done the honourable thing but his skills would have been retained. But it is doubtful if the urbane Carrington, described by one journal as 'amiable and popular', would have been the man to stand up to the pressures which developed during April and May.

He was too fastidious, too languid for the hard decisions to be made. Given unlimited time, Carrington was a skilful negotiator; perhaps, when he resigned, he had the intelligence to take this limitation into account. He insisted on going, perhaps as much influenced by apprehension for the future as guilt about the past. A sensitive man, he knew that while he stayed his presence would become an increasing source of bitterness and tension within his party.

Carrington's deputy, Humphrey Atkins and a junior Foreign Office Minister, Richard Luce, resigned with him. In his letter of resignation Carrington said, 'The invasion of the Falklands has been a humiliating affront to this country'. Virtually everybody felt this humiliation and it was significantly non-party. Labour members, in their anger over the humiliation, said that it had been inflicted by a 'tin-pot dictator' and a 'two-bit Mussolini'. Mrs Thatcher appointed Francis Pym, the leading contender for Conservative leadership, with a wide following and the ability to inspire loyalty as the new Foreign Secretary. Mr John Nott, the Defence Secretary, badly shaken by the Falklands invasion, twice offered to resign but Mrs Thatcher refused the offer. She was right to do so because throughout the pre-crisis period the Ministry of Defence was not the architect of policy, merely the agency by which it was executed. Even the naval cuts were not the fault of Mr Nott alone but reflected the priorities of the Prime Minister. Unspectacular as a leader – despite having been an officer of the Gurkhas – he is nevertheless a sound arranger and organiser.

Britain took the crisis to the United Nations Security Council on 3 April. Ten members declared Argentina to be an aggressor and, in Resolution 502, demanded an immediate withdrawal; Panama opposed the resolution, while the Soviet Union, Poland, China and Spain abstained. The Soviet and Polish votes were predictable and reflected anti-British feeling rather than pro-Argentinian sentiments. Spain has racial and linguistic links with Argentina and Panama always reacts violently to anything labelled 'colonialism' and Britain was allegedly guilty of just this. Argentina, apparently, was not colonising when it invaded the Falklands. A Security Council resolution is supposed to be mandatory, not a basis for discussion. The Argentinians ignored it.

Another early British diplomatic success was the

unanimous decision by the EEC countries to support Britain and to condemn the Argentinian action – and to punish it by trade sanctions. The Europeans announced an embargo on arms and military spare parts; they also decided to ban all imports from Argentina, which amount to about 1.76 billion dollars a year. Even more important, NATO gave Britain its moral backing and sustained its support.

Mrs Thatcher simply *assumed* that she would be helped by the Reagan administration. Britain has been the firmest U.S. ally throughout the twentieth century. Whenever the U.S. has asked for similar kinds of help from its friends Britain has given it, often at considerable cost. In recent years the Thatcher government has joined in U.S. sponsored sanctions against the Soviet Union for its invasion of Afghanistan, endorsed the U.S. call for a boycott of the 1980 Olympics and trenchantly criticised the martial-law regime in Poland. Britain supported sanctions against Iran during the U.S. embassy hostage crisis and Mrs Thatcher has constantly supported the U.S. nuclear build-up to counter increased Soviet strategic forces; this support included the unpopular decision to base U.S. Cruise missiles on British soil. If Mrs Thatcher had been deliberately paying instalments on an insurance policy she could not have better arranged her nation's security. Reagan might delay giving help, he could not refuse it.

From the beginning British diplomacy was direct and pragmatic. The British Ambassador in Washington, Sir Nicholas Henderson, told U.S. Secretary of State Alexander Haig, 'American interests are at stake as much as ours. If it's a question of overthrowing frontiers and sovereignty and territorial integrity by force in the American hemisphere goodness knows where it will end ... If U.S. territory were occupied or assaulted, as it has been, you wouldn't start negotiating until the military situation had been restored. The U.S. did not sit down with Japan the day after Pearl Harbor.'

With such simple but powerful arguments it was only to be expected that the British would carry the Americans with them, although one State Department official said that the U.S. did not wish to help in the overthrow of the Argentine generals for a 150-year-old 'pimple on the ass' – his reference to the Falklands. And the Defence Department announced: 'The U.S. is right down the middle of the Falklands dispute.'

The Reagan administration was 'right down the middle' only in that it faced the horns of a dilemma, knowing that it would certainly be impaled on one of them. It would be impossible to maintain ties with its oldest and staunchest ally without damaging its budding friendship with Argentina, a country that the U.S. hopes will help its campaign to prevent the spread of communism in the Western Hemisphere. 'It is a very difficult situation for the U.S.' the President said, 'because we're friends with both countries engaged in this dispute.' Such public ambivalence during the first weeks of the crisis gave the unfortunate impression that he could not choose between Britain and the country that not only was the aggressor but had also a bloody history of human rights violations. Herblock, the cartoonist, commenting on Reagan's initial reaction not to take sides, drew a harassed official saying to the President, 'Right chief – we stick to a middle course between sound judgment and complete idiocy.'

On the day the Argentinians stormed Port Stanley the Argentinian ambassador in Washington, Estaban Takacs, gave a dinner at which the guest of honour was the U.S. Ambassador, Jeane Kirkpatrick and with her was Deputy-Secretary of State Walter Stoessel, the most senior U.S. career diplomat. The timing was no accident; as the C.I.A. was later to discover the Argentinians had been planning the invasion for two months and Takacs knew of it. The dinner was a stratagem designed to give the impression that friction between the U.S. and Argentina was unlikely.

The Argentinian campaign to win over Ambassador Kirkpatrick was remarkably successful. She had already said that the Argentinian regime was an example of a 'friendly authoritarian' government in the hemisphere. Now, during a meeting of the National Security Planning Group (the inner circle of the United States' National Security Council) to consider the Falklands, Mrs Kirkpatrick argued strongly that the U.S. should 'respect the sensitivities of the nationalistic Argentinians'. The Falklands issue, she said, must not undermine the American interest in building up a common anti-Communist front among Latin Americans. Throughout the next six hectic weeks of negotiation Mrs Kirkpatrick was conspicuously silent – but she was to be vehemently outspoken later about vicious sexist abuse of Mrs Thatcher in the U.N. Security Council.

Desperately engaged in a balancing act, President Reagan sent Secretary of State Alexander Haig flying to London and Buenos Aires, searching as an 'honest broker' for a peaceful solution. After London he announced that he was 'highly impressed by the firm determination of the British Government'. Next day in Buenos Aires he spent a total of eleven hours in talks with President Galtieri and other Argentinian leaders.

These talks produced some 'specific ideas' which he took back to London. The Argentine Foreign Minister, Nicanor Costa Mendez, announced at the time that he was 'very optimistic' that a peaceful settlement could be found, while through a spokesman the White House said, 'We think there are reasonable prospects for a settlement.'

In five more hours of talks with Haig, Mrs Thatcher made the British position clear. She told him, 'Stop talking about American evenhandedness and tell the Junta to obey the Security Council resolution to withdraw its forces. Only after this happens will we be prepared to talk about the future of the islands'.

In her conduct of the Falklands affair from the moment of the invasion Mrs Thatcher was driven by strong human and political emotion. But suggestions that she was bellicose and inflexible were wrong. Nor was she thinking only of retaining political power at all costs; all her words and actions suggested that she had risen above party politics for the duration of the conflict. That she was affected by patriotism can hardly be questioned but there was little in her language that hinted of narrow nationalism. During the negotiations, parliamentary debates and numerous interviews which were to follow in the next seven weeks Mrs Thatcher showed herself to be a patient, humane and reasonable person, certainly with a strong will, but also a willingness to listen.

When her own resignation was demanded in Parliament Mrs Thatcher said crisply, 'No. Now is the time for strength and resolution.' The implication was clear – only she could provide this amalgum. Foreign Secretary Pym said, equally crisply, 'Britain does not appease dictators.' And his meaning was also clear – do not expect Margaret Thatcher to weaken on this matter of principle.

Mrs Thatcher had public opinion behind her to a greater extent than any Prime Minister facing an international crisis, other than when Churchill rallied the British people during the dangerous days of mid-1940 as Britain stood alone against the Nazi-Fascist Axis. A public opinion poll showed eighty-three per cent in favour of regaining the Falklands and fifty-three per cent preferred the use of force and this percentage was to increase.

All those involved in the negotiations were expressing a wish and a hope rather than expectation or conviction. Whatever concessions the British Government might make, there was never any likelihood that the Argentinians would remove their troops from the Falklands or reduce the strength of their demands for sovereignty over them. Margaret Thatcher was saying, over and again, that any Falklands settlement would have to be acceptable to the islanders, the British Parliament and British people.

Her insistent energy produced rapid, sustained action. By 5 April the light aircraft carriers *Hermes* and *Invincible* – strictly speaking not aircraft carriers at all but floating platforms – and about twenty-eight other ships had left Portsmouth and were heading south, the first of a steady flow of ships which would soon constitute Britain's biggest military expedition since the Second World War. The preparation and sailing of this fleet within four days showed political incisiveness and was a considerable military achievement.

Not everybody would agree with this view. In the *Washington Post*, columnist Stephen Rosenfeld stated: 'The question will linger of whether Mrs Thatcher did what had to be done or went to military excess. The decision to dispatch the fleet could not have been taken more carelessly. Thatcher and Parliament, in a patriotic fervour, whooped it through on the very day after the Argentinians took the islands. Scarcely a soul gave thought to what was being set in train. We have a passion for "lessons" and now conduct our post-mortems even before there has been a mortem, but the lesson of the fleet's precipitate dispatch seems to rate central attention, whatever happens now.'

Rosenfeld's assumptions are made carelessly, but there was nothing careless about the decision to send the fleet. This was clear, look-ahead thinking. Mrs Thatcher and her advisers knew the risks and dangers that lay ahead; they knew too that if they did *not* at once send the fleet an interminable, fruitless war of words at the U.N. or a protracted shooting war would take place. To the military analyst and to the political scientist the 'precipitate dispatch' certainly deserves central attention, as Rosenfeld suggests – but as an example of incisive purpose in defence of a principle.

Mrs Thatcher put aside any idea of defeat. 'Failure?' she said in a television interview. 'The possibilities do not exist. I'm not talking about failure. I am talking about supreme confidence in the British fleet, superlative troops, excellent equipment. We must use all our professionalism, our flair, every single bit of native cunning and all our equipment. We must go out calmly, quietly, to succeed.'

British and world reaction startled the Argentinians but in no way put them off course; even American pressure, applied at that time, could not reverse the Argentine decision. President Reagan tried. He warned Galtieri, by telephone, that Mrs Thatcher was 'a determined person who could not be expected to accept' Argentinian takeover of the Falklands. It was by then too late.

Pressure grew within the U.S. Congress for the Reagan administration to side more openly with Britain. The Senate voted seventy-nine to one in favour of a pro-British resolution that called on the U.S. Government to 'use all appropriate means to assist the British government'. While Congress and Senate were applying this pressure Haig cabled his final settlement proposals directly to the U.S. ambassador to Argentina to be placed before the Junta. Two days later in came the reply through Estaban Takacs: the answer was 'No'. President Reagan and his Secretary of State, rebuffed as go-betweens, now made it plain that they backed Britain. Mrs Thatcher's assumption that this would happen was proved correct.

President Galtieri has been compared with the U.S.

World War II General George S. Patton and former Argentine president Juan Peron, with whom he shares a fondness for addressing crowds from the balcony of the Casa Rosade, the presidential palace. Galtieri likes the comparison and this is significant. Patton was an inflexible, insensitive, flamboyant general who resented criticism and liked to say that he could 'lick the Germans' on his own. Peron was a vainglorious, chauvinistic and self-centred man who brushed aside all counsel. Patton rarely used 'if' and 'but' and Galtieri is noted for the same direct uncompromising approach.

In Galtieri's view ordinary politicians often stand in the way of Argentina's ambitions. 'We don't want to be a country,' he told an American journalist, 'we want to be a great country. The Argentine problem is that there has not been a political solution to any problem in fifty years ... The ballot boxes are well stored away and they will remain well stored away.'

The world was watching, fascinated by the spectacle of two nations, separated by 8,000 miles of ocean, preparing to fight each other. In every respect it would be an unusual war and the world's press and people had sensed this. *Time* magazine considered that the Falklands were perhaps the most bizarre place for an armed conflict since the Orcs attacked J. R. Tolkien's Middle-Earth. More seriously, it was a war between democracy and despotism and piracy and law, between old principles and new opportunism, between (in historic terms) a veteran nation and an upstart, between a woman of will and a man of wilfulness. In addition there were unknown factors, such as the use of new weapons, previously untried in war.

On 12 April Galtieri told a cheering crowd, 'If the British want to come, let them come. We will take them on. We will inflict punishment on anyone who dares to touch one metre of Argentinian soil.'

The British did come on.

4 Men and Microchips

The public's farewell to the Fleet at Portsmouth was reminiscent of the departure of the Army and the Navy to the Boer War, 1899–1902. British people have always gathered at Portsmouth Harbour to see the Fleet sail but nobody present when *Invincible* and *Hermes*, the flagship, swept past could recall such an emotion-laden occasion. The spectators, some of whom had been weeping moments before, waved Union flags and held placards reading GOOD LUCK and UK - OK. Sailors in their blue and white dress uniforms dressed ship in the traditional farewell. Small boats packed with spectators bobbed in the wake of the big ships.

The decks of *Invincible* and *Hermes* were stacked with munitions, vertical take-off Harrier attack aircraft and Sea King helicopters. Just over 2,000 Royal Marine Commandos, the spearhead of the assault group, were also aboard the ships.

Once out in the Atlantic the carriers were joined by destroyers, frigates and support vessels until the fleet numbered nearly thirty before long: it would soon rise to sixty. Running at night under blackout conditions, these ships formed the largest British military armada since the Second World War. Far ahead of the surface ships, the submarines, some of them nuclear-powered, were already prowling the waters around the Falklands.

These submarines were to be the enforcers of the blockade, but they have no halfway measure of enforcement. They can either fire their wire-guided Tigerfish torpedoes, which could destroy any ship in the Argentinian fleet, or they can do nothing but watch through the periscope and act as an early warning system.

The Royal Navy's full strength at the outbreak of hostilities was two light carriers, fourteen destroyers, forty-six frigates, twelve nuclear-powered submarines, sixteen conventional submarines and four Polaris-armed submarines. This was a dramatic shrinking from the 586 vessels with which Britain finished the war of 1939–45 but the Royal Navy is still the world's third largest. It was designed though to fight a different kind of war from that in the South Atlantic. For twenty years British defence policy has been to shape its military face to the NATO mould. That meant defending Britain itself, contributing to the central front in Germany and having a navy that could keep the Atlantic sea lanes open. The liberation fleet soon adapted itself to its new role.

In addition to the warships already under way the government requisitioned three British Petroleum tankers to serve as fuel transports. The Navy was already drawing heavily on the Royal Fleet Auxiliary Service, whose twenty-four ships belong to the Defence Ministry but whose officers and crew are technically members of the British merchant marine.

The educational cruise-ship *Uganda* was taken over and, in Gibraltar, rapidly turned into a thousand-bed hospital ship. Simultaneously the knowledge of British doctors with the most thorough experience of gunshot and shell splinter wounds was being put together by task force medical staff. All the skills of surgeons and other specialists at the Royal Victoria Hospital, Belfast, where treatment of bombing and shooting victims is commonplace, were quickly put into report form for the expedition's doctors.

At Southampton, the 45,000-ton 1,600-passenger cruise ship *Canberra* became a troop and supply ship. She was stripped of her heavy fittings, chandeliers and heavy curtains; two helicopter pads were fitted onto the liner's decks, one of them across an empty swimming pool. Rations, munitions, armoured vehicles, guns, and other equipment were loaded and 2,000 Royal Marines and men of the Parachute Regiment – both élite formations – were marched aboard. Thirty nurses accompanied the troops in case the *Canberra* became a hospital ship. Many members of the *Canberra*'s crew volunteered for duty in the South Atlantic; there was solid financial inducement to do so – ordinary seamen would get their usual £150 a week as far as Ascension Island and after that £400.

As the task force ploughed steadily south the fighting men were practising. Pilots of the Harriers made simulated combat flights and skimmed the waves to avoid radar detection. Under orders, they fired some of their weapons close to the carriers to accustom the crews to the noise of combat. Helicopter crews worked non-stop for hours at a time to perfect their tricky approaches and landings; the margin between perfection and disaster on a heaving ship in rough water is narrow, as was to be tragically demonstrated later. Marines had a timetable of physical training and weapons practice.

Admiral Woodward and his senior officers, army and navy, were already planning the use of the formidable array of electronic warfare equipment. Officers could 'listen' to the enemy's radar and tell from them where he was and what he was doing. They could also jam enemy radar with strong counter-beams and even feed them with false signals. Most Argentine missiles were built in Britain and the Navy thought they knew how they could be thrown off course. Above all, the sophisticated electronics possessed by the Fleet would be able to jam all messages between the Falklands and the mainland, though there might be times when it was useful to allow certain information to get through.

The computered, microchip weapons to be used in the impending fighting were formidable and their real destructive effect could only be guessed at, since many of them had not before been used in war. The arsenal of the electronic age was to be tested in action. Whatever the distress and dread of ordinary people, military strategists and weapons makers all over the world waited in fascinated anticipation. The Soviet naval command was particularly interested.

They were watching to see the effect of advanced radar and bombing computers, American heat-seeking Sidewinder air-to-air missiles, anti-personnel scatter bombs, Tigerfish torpedoes steered to their target by computer signals transmitted along their guidance wires, the British Skyflash air-to-air, the Blowpipe, Bloodhound and Rapier ground-to-air

35

missile systems, the American 'Smart' bomb which homes on a laser beam shone on to the target by a spotter aircraft.

Then there was Sea Wolf, an extremely fast short-range missile with radar or television guidance capable of shooting down a shell in flight, and Sea Skua air-to-sea missiles. A sausage-shaped device, 8-ft long and weighing 165 lbs, the Sea Skua had been in Royal Navy service for less than a year. Designed for helicopter launch, the missile has a range of about nine miles, greater than that of the anti-aircraft weapons sent against it. To use it, a helicopter pilot flies close enough to let its radar light up the target with radio energy; when reflected, this provides a starting guide for the missile's homing computer. The Sea Skua streaks to the target at 550 mph, only six feet above the surface; then it explodes after penetration, to create maximum damage.

The French weapons makers were hoping to see the first use in war of their Exocet AM 39 missile, a 15.5 ft, 1,140 lb air-to-sea missile. Both the British and Argentine navies have Exocets, which cost £110,000 each. The air version can be launched by a plane flying as high as 33,000 ft or as low as 300 ft. The pilot simply programmes the Exocet's computer with range and bearing of the target; when the plane is between thirty-seven and forty-three miles from target the pilot launches the missile and flies home. The Exocet drops to the surface and skims about 8 ft above even the roughest waves and just below the speed of sound. Eight miles from target, the missile's radar system takes over and steers it towards the enemy ship.

The weapon likely to be fired most frequently was the Royal Navy's Vickers 4.5-inch gun, shooting 50-lb shells at a rate of twenty-five a minute. The latest version is the fully automatic single-barrelled Mark 8 developed from the Army's Abbott self-propelled gun. The Mark 8 has a range of about thirteen miles and came into service first on the light cruiser H.M.S. *Bristol*, part of the task force. After that it was fitted to the Type 42 destroyers; *Coventry* and *Glasgow*, and Type 21 Amazon class frigates; *Arrow*, *Alacrity* and *Antelope*. Two County class destroyers, *Antrim* and *Glamorgan*, and the Rothesay class frigates *Plymouth* and *Yarmouth* are equipped with the twin-barrelled Mark 6 4.5 gun.

As the Fleet sailed south, air support was flying to Ascension Island, a British colony, 3,340 miles from the Falklands. Among the planes were Nimrods, mainly reconnaissance aircraft but armed with torpedoes and 'Smart' target-seeking bombs; Nimrods have a range of 5,755 miles and can be refuelled in the air. Then there were the C-130 Hercules military transports, ready for use when the Falklands were retaken. Finally, the twenty-year-old but still formidable Vulcan bombers, which could reach the Falklands from Ascension and, with a mid-air refuelling, return.

The first brush between enemies occurred when an Argentinian reconnaissance plane loaded with electronic gear came within twelve miles of the fleet, only to be warded off by a Harrier. The pilot was still reluctant to open fire; the British flier, Simon Hargreaves, said, 'I had live Sidewinders locked on him. If I had fired he would have been dead, but I wouldn't like to have been responsible for starting a war.'

The success of the liberation fleet rested heavily on the shoulders of Rear-Admiral John ('Sandy') Woodward. A man of quiet, reflective manner, he had had four sea-going commands before being appointed flag officer of the First Flotilla in August 1981. His first command was as captain of the submarine H.M.S. *Tireless*; later he commanded two other submarines, H.M.S. *Grampus* and H.M.S. *Warspite* and in 1977 he was moved to H.M.S. *Sheffield*; the first sea-trials of the Sea Dart missile system took place in H.M.S. *Sheffield* when Woodward was captain. The British peace-time navy has only three sea-going admirals and his selection as task force commander was virtually automatic. Rear-Admiral Derek Reffell, flag officer of the Third Flotilla – which includes the carriers *Hermes* and *Invincible* – had only just taken over from Vice-Admiral John Cox, who went to Naval Air Command. Woodward, with nine months seniority, was clearly in line for the Falklands mission. While at sea the Admiral learned that in the latest Service pay increases he was to get an extra £3,065 a year, taking his salary to £25,000.

He would certainly be earning his money. He did not know when he left Portsmouth – there had been no time for detailed briefings – that Mrs Thatcher and her cabinet wanted the war, if it had to come, to be over by mid-June. They had several reasons. After that time real winter would have arrived, making even movement on foot difficult; if the fighting went on beyond mid-June Argentina might be able to find fighting and not just talking allies, or at least friends who would supply planes and ships.

Few people realised just how delicate Admiral Woodward's task was – or that he would be judged on two aspects of leadership. The first is the obvious one: could he achieve his objective with minimum loss to his own forces? The second factor is a new one in warfare and has arisen from the contorted diplomacy of the post-colonial world. He would have to keep the vast fire-power of his forces to a politically acceptable minimum; that is, he could not simply blaze away and kill large numbers of Argentinian troops – even after Galtieri had announced that he and the nation were prepared to accept 40,000 dead Argentinians in the coming war.

Not that the Argentinians expected him to be able to achieve much against them. One of their leading newspapers observed that 'Sandy is an absurd name; how can anybody named "Sandy" be a good admiral?'

Some of the faster ships of the armada, which was moving at eighteen knots, had raced ahead to South Georgia, whose early capture could have powerful psychological and strategic advantages for the British.

The first troops ashore were about twelve men of the Special Boat Service (S.B.S), put ashore the previous Thursday by a submarine. Then came fifteen men of the 22nd Special Air Service Regiment (S.A.S.) flown by a helicopter onto the Fortuna Glacier. They were to observe the Argentinian positions, and then prepare the ground for the arrival of the assault troops. The hardy S.A.S. men found conditions too extreme even for them, with icy 100 mph winds making movement impossible. Aware of their plight the captain of the covering warship, HMS *Antrim*, sent in a Mark V Wessex helicopter to bring the men out; in the appalling conditions on the glacier the plane crashed a few seconds after take-off with the S.A.S. men. A second helicopter was called in and it too crashed. A third attempt was made by Lieutenant-Commander Ian Stanley and by remarkably skilful flying he brought out the S.A.S. men and the crews of the crashed helicopter in a single flight; for this heroic feat and others he was later awarded the Distinguished Service Order.

Undaunted by their ordeal and setback, the S.A.S. men set out in five Gemini rubber boats to reach the mainland. The engine on one failed almost at once and the howling wind carried the Gemini away, with nobody able to do a thing to save the three men aboard. A second boat was also blown away but a searching helicopter pilot saw its emergency beacon next morning and rescued the S.A.S. men. The other three boats reached shore and radioed that there seemed to be about a hundred Argentinian defenders, acting in a lax and unsuspecting manner.

On Sunday 25 April* navy helicopters sighted the Argentine submarine, *Santa Fé*, a former American vessel bought in 1971, and attacked it. Foremost in this attack were Lieutenant-Commander Stanley and

* Historically this was a significant day for a military landing; on 25 April 1915 Australian, New Zealand and British troops had landed under fire on the Gallipoli peninsula, Turkey. The parallel ends there. By the end of the year the British force withdrew after suffering 45,000 casualties. The 1982 landing was quickly successful.

Lieutenant-Commander John Ellerbeck, later awarded the D.S.C..

Damaged by rockets and machine-gun fire the *Santa Fé* ran herself aground on the beach in Grytviken Harbour. As about fifty Argentinian troops scrambled from the stricken submarine the British saw that they had intercepted reinforcements for the garrison. The Navy had plans for a bombardment of the Argentine positions followed by a conventional landing. But aboard H.M.S. *Antrim* the S.A.S. squadron commander suggested an immediate thrust to capitalise on the destruction of the submarine. The idea was taken up and Major Guy Sheridan of the Royal Marines led thirty S.A.S. men in a daring raid through a minefield. It was the best type of operation – one accomplished so efficiently that the enemy offered no resistance. The S.A.S. men ran up the Union flag on the flagstaff. The garrison at Leith, twenty-six miles away, was given a chance to surrender – by radio – but declined. They would fight to the last man, they said. They changed their minds quickly the following morning when S.A.S. men, supported by Royal Marines, arrived with the same brisk no-nonsense manner they had shown at Grytviken. Together the S.A.S. and Marines captured 156 soldiers and sailors and thirty-eight civilians in the South Georgia operation. The only man wounded was a *Santa Fé* sailor whose leg was later amputated by a British navy surgeon. Another Argentinian later died during what was called 'a serious incident'. The S.A.S. men – and their comrades in arms of the S.B.S. who had also landed on South Georgia – were soon en route to the

Falklands. The work of these splendid men, intelligent, brave and resourceful, is described later in the book.

Admiral Woodward's signal to Admiralty concerning the recapture of South Georgia was traditional in its language. It began 'Be pleased to inform Her Majesty ...' and ended 'God save the Queen'. Mrs Thatcher needed the South Georgia victory even more than the Queen did, and appearing on television that evening, she urged her people to 'Rejoice, rejoice!' She compared the British handling of the Falklands crisis with her government's handling of the hijacked Tanzanian aircraft which had landed at Stansted Airport; the British refused to let the aircraft take off again. 'That's the way to stop hijacking,' Mrs Thatcher said. 'Similarly, to see that an invader does not succeed is to stop further invasions and to really stand up for international law against international anarchy'. Next day, after the raid, the House of Commons greeted Mrs Thatcher with a roar of approval.

As is common in the first stages of wars, the victors in South Georgia were magnanimous; the commanders of the *Santa Fé* and the garrison were entertained by dinner aboard a British ship. The British officers did not know at the time that the commander of the garrison was the infamous Captain Alfredo Astiz, known as 'Captain Death', one of the chief torturers and executioners of the military regime.

The initial Argentinian reaction to the retaking of South Georgia was to claim that the landing had not taken place, the first of many bizarre statements to flash from Buenos Aires in the propaganda war. Then the Argentinian Government said that the British landing was 'an open declaration of war' and called for help from its Latin American allies. They said, in effect, that they would weep for Argentina – nothing more.

Winning back South Georgia, which is one hundred miles long, provided the British fleet with a beachhead and staging area that it badly needed at such a great distance from its home ports. Even so, Grytviken is 800 miles from the Falklands.

On 12 April the British had declared a 200-mile 'maritime exclusion zone' around the Falklands. Taking this threat to their communications seriously, the Argentinian command worked continuously to reinforce the garrison by air, using nine C-130 Hercules transports and two civilian airliners to land 800 tons of food and equipment daily. Galtieri made a one-day visit to Port Stanley, newly named Puerto Argentino, and in a speech to the troops said, 'The Argentine flag will continue to fly. All necessary defence measures have been taken.' Realistically, the Argentinians could not have hoped to guard the Falklands adequately even with 50,000 troops, let alone 9,000.

Admiral Woodward was also talking. In a briefing given to journalists aboard the flagship, H.M.S. *Hermes*, he declared his intention to make the Falklands blockade air and sea tight, using the twenty jump-jet Harriers with the task force. He had another eighteen on the way in a container ship. After the victory on South Georgia the Admiral had permitted himself some comments which were no more characteristic of the Silent Service than they were of himself. 'Now the heavy punch is coming behind. This is the run-up to the big match, which, in my view, should be a walkover.' To the Argentinian troops on the Falklands, he added, 'If you want to get out, I suggest you do so now. Once we arrive the only way home will be courtesy of the Royal Navy.'

This language, reminiscent of General Bernard Montgomery 'hitting the Germans for six right out of Africa,' was too ebullient for the Admiralty, where Woodward's superiors chided him. Mrs Thatcher referred in a barbed way to the 'Admiral's vivid speech'.

It is likely that the Admiral was speaking to his men, who would expect him to use such gung-ho terms; probably a journalist overheard him and presented the colourful passage as an interview. No politician himself, the Admiral, in a mixed state of tension and euphoria, miscalculated the likely effect of his words.

Later Admiral Woodward reversed his earlier confident talk and warned that the conflict could turn into 'a long and bloody campaign'. This was no more popular in Whitehall than his earlier announcement and after that he had little to say.

Meanwhile the Argentinian military governor, Menendez, was trying to induce Falkland Islanders to leave their islands. Before the blockade made any further departures impossible about twenty permanent residents left; another seventy or eighty, on long term contract, also left. On the evening of Wednesday 14 April, Defence Secretary John Nott warned that the Royal Navy would sink any

Argentine vessel, whether warship or merchantman, that was within 200 miles of the islands after midnight on Sunday 28 April. 'We will shoot first,' Nott said. 'We will sink them.' The Argentinians had responded to the earlier maritime blockade with a 200 mile exclusion zone of their own – taken together, the British and Argentinian announcements were tacit declarations of war.

This was very clear to Secretary of State Haig who said, on 30 April, 'The South Atlantic crisis is about to enter a new and dangerous phase in which large-scale military action is likely.' It was the moment he chose to announce the the time had come for the U.S. to abandon its neutral 'down the middle' position; from that moment the U.S. would provide whatever supplies the British wanted and would join fourteen other Western nations in imposing economic sanctions against Argentina. This meant that Argentina could no longer buy military stores and munitions and was barred from credits and loans.

With the warships in position around the Falklands, the task force was attempting to choke off supplies to the occupation army. The big ships were only ninety miles offshore, being guarded by anti-submarine frigates and the nuclear-powered hunter-killer submarines; destroyers interposed themselves between the islands and the mainland to establish a radar picket about one hundred miles west of the Falklands. For days on end winds of up to fifty miles-an-hour whipped up forty-foot waves; sometimes the propellors of the lighter ships were spinning in mid-air.

The blockade strategy was hampered from the

start by inadequate air cover. While the Harriers are highly manoeuvrable, they are relatively slow at 736 mph. Also, they had a maximum range of only 460 miles – or about one hundred miles for a thirty-minute patrol. The Royal Navy's version of the Harrier is not ideal for supporting ground troops; for that the longer range R.A.F. version of the Harrier, the GR Mk3, was needed.

Even with the R.A.F. Harriers, the British were outgunned in the air. The Argentinians had eighty-two American-made A-4P and A-4Q Skyhawk attack aircraft, twenty-one French-built Mirage, 111 fighter-bombers and twenty-six Dagger aircraft, the Israeli Mirage-type aircraft. The Argentine Mirage 111s have a combat range of about 745 miles, enabling them to operate over the Falklands from mainland bases, but for extremely short periods.

The opening shots in Admiral Woodward's 'big match' were fired on Saturday 1 May. A crisp announcement from the Ministry of Defence confirmed what the world had steadily come to fear – war. In a spate of attacks British aircraft swept in over Port Stanley and struck at the 4,000-ft airstrip. First came a long-range delta-winged Vulcan bomber from the Ascension Island base, 3,340 miles away. The Vulcan refuelled in the air on its way to the target, dropped twenty-one half-ton bombs and, according to a Defence Ministry spokesman, left the runway severely cratered, probably using the new JP233 airfield attack bomb. The result of collaboration between British and U.S. firms, the JP233 craters the runways by penetrating the concrete before exploding; the surface then lifts and breaks

46

over a wide area. The same bomb also seeds the area with delayed-action anti-personnel explosives. It is possible too that the British used the 610-lb BL 755 cluster bomb for the first time; this destroys armour and thin-skinned targets and strews the area with smaller bombs timed to explode at intervals.

About three hours after the Vulcan raid on Port Stanley airport, carrier-based Sea Harrier jets armed with 1,000-lb bombs and cannons swooped in again on the airfield. In a separate attack, Harriers attacked a grassy airfield fifty miles away, near Goose Green. British warships shelled the airfield and other military installations. In a final smaller attack a Sea King helicopter strafed Argentinian positions near Darwin, close to Goose Green.

While the air attacks were going on, British warships were also shelling the airport, supply and fuel dumps. The combined assault virtually destroyed Argentina's ability to resupply its troops, then believed to be 9,000. It also greatly eased the task of protecting the task force, now made up of more than sixty ships. But protection, without much more air cover, could not be guaranteed.

Requested to surrender, the Argentinian commander on the Falklands replied over his radio, 'Nonsense – we're winning.' And he added, 'Bring on the little Prince,' – a reference to Prince Andrew, a helicopter pilot on H.M.S. *Invincible.*

The Argentinian propaganda machine was soon claiming counter strikes; seven British planes had been shot down. But B.B.C. reporters who counted out the raiding British aeroplanes counted the same number back. The Argentinians sent six Israeli-built

Dagger jets against the fleet and slightly damaged a frigate and wounded one sailor – the first naval casualty.

By early May about 4,000 marines and paratroopers were with the task force, 2,500 of them aboard the converted liner *Canberra*. During the first week of May another 1,200 troops left for the battle zone aboard the *Norland* ferry.

The battle zone, frigid in weather, was hotting up in military expectation.

5 In Hot Blood and Cold Blood

A good many people saw the British–Argentine conflict, even up to the bombing of the Falkland airstrips, as a display of posturing belligerence and retaliatory belligerence – bluff and double bluff. The first air combat engagement on 2 May gave a hint that serious action was imminent. A Navy Sea Harrier flown by an R.A.F. pilot, Flight-Lieutenant Bertie Penfold, intercepted an Argentine Mirage closing on the fleet and shot it down with a Sidewinder missile; Penfold's was the first jump-jet to take part in combat. Much more serious incidents on 3 May and 4 May finally blew away illusions about the nature of the war.

About thirty-six miles outside the total exclusion zone were the Argentine cruiser, *General Belgrano*, 13,645 tons, and two escorting destroyers. Armed with fifteen six-inch and five-inch guns and surface to air Seacat missiles, the *Belgrano*, though of World War II vintage, had more firepower than any ship of the British fleet. For some days the nuclear-powered submarine H.M.S. *Conqueror*, whose commander was Captain Richard Wraith, had been shadowing the *Belgrano*. The cruiser and the destroyers skirted the edge of the exclusion zone and crossed into it at least once. Then the *Belgrano* changed course and made towards the British task force. Wraith flashed the information to Admiral Woodward, who passed it on to Admiral of the Fleet Sir Terence Lewin, Chief of Defence Staff, in London. Lewin went personally to No 10 Downing Street, where the War Cabinet was meeting. He recommended that *Conqueror* should 'act to defend the fleet'.

This decision taken, back to Wraith went the order to fire. Two wire-guided Tigerfish torpedoes sped from the submarine. About twenty-one feet long and weighing 3,400-lbs, the Tigerfish has a range of twenty miles – though *Conqueror* was much closer than this. After launching, they raced towards their target at nearly sixty mph, paying out thin wires attached to the submarine's computer. In the final stages, when the computer had determined that the torpedoes were heading in the right direction, the automatic homing system took over. The Tigerfish is superquiet and the *Belgrano*'s crew could have had no warning of the attack.

Stricken, the *Belgrano* stayed afloat for forty minutes and then disappeared from British and Argentine radar screens to become the largest ship sunk in a naval action since American attacks in the Inland Sea of Japan in 1945. The escorting destroyers had left the big ship and at first report only 125 members of the *Belgrano*'s crew were said to have survived, but in all 800 were rescued; 368 were lost.

At first Buenos Aires denied the sinking, saying it was a British psychological warfare lie, but with the large numbers of survivors the pretence could not be sustained. Buenos Aires then called the attack a 'treacherous act of armed aggression'. The official British reaction was that it could not risk allowing the

Belgrano to use its guns against the British fleet. Treachery was an irrelevance; in announcing the exclusion zone Britain had made it clear that its forces would be free to defend themselves and to attack potential attackers *outside* the zone. Also, Britain had declared a 200-mile defensive circle around its task force. The Argentine Government had been notified of all these British restrictions.

The Royal Navy was in no doubt that it had taken the correct course. The *Belgrano*'s sinking was announced over Tannoy systems throughout the fleet and the men nodded their understanding. British seamen might applaud the bringing down of an enemy aircraft but they never cheer when a ship is sunk. When *Hermes*' executive officer, Commander James Locke, announced the death of the Argentine cruiser his voice was almost regretful.

Argentina suffered another naval reverse. A patrol ship, the *Sobral*, was hit by a missile from a Lynx helicopter and sunk and a second patrol boat badly damaged.

With the Argentinians reeling from loss of the *Belgrano* – it was an immense blow to their prestige – the British sent further Harrier bombing attacks against the airstrips at Port Stanley and Goose Green. During one of these raids the British admitted their first loss, a Sea Harrier shot down near Goose Green; the pilot Lieutenant Nicholas Taylor, was killed. The first British casualty of the war had been Able Seaman Ian Britnell, a missile gunner, hit by shell splinters during a raid on his frigate, *Alacrity*.

It was clear from the debate in the House of Commons on 4 May, which was largely about the sinking of the *Belgrano*, that many MPs still did not understand the reality of war. Typical was the Liberal Leader, David Steel, who asked the Defence Secretary for confirmation that military action was still measured and controlled. 'Is there an instruction to the fleet that all action must be taken only if totally unavoidable?' he asked. Mr Nott, nonplussed by Mr Steel's ignorance of war, could only reply that it was clear that the orders to the Argentine fleet were to sink British ships.

He could have told Mr Steel that the instruction he wanted would make commanders impotent or so delay their response – while they pondered whether it was 'totally unavoidable' – that they put their own men in danger.

The military necessity of immediate response – and if possible of pre-emptive response – may have been demonstrated to Mr Steel and others by the next horrific episode of the war. On 4 May – the same day as the House of Commons debate – H.M.S. *Sheffield* (the 'Shiny Sheff') was on radar patrol about seventy miles west of the Falklands and fifteen miles from the rest of the fleet. She was on station to give warning of any Argentine attack that might threaten the vulnerable aircraft carriers. Three Argentine French-built fighters, including at least one Super Etendard fighter-bomber, were in the air about 550 miles from their base at Rio Gallegos. The 'Action Stations!' alarm sounded on *Invincible* and the crew were told: 'Air raid imminent from the south-west. Two aircraft at sixty miles and closing.' But in that direction, between *Invincible* and the planes, was *Sheffield*. (Captain 'Sam' Salt.)

Captain Augusto Cesar Vedacarratz, at the age of thirty-seven perhaps Argentina's top pilot, was flying one of the Super Etendards. His radar picked up the *Sheffield* and locked on. About thirty miles from the ship Vedacarratz and another pilot fired an Exocet each – at radar blips rather than at the ship visually – and then dived away without observing the results. Vedacarratz did not know what he had done until the Ministry of Defence announced it in London.

The Bridge saw the missile when it was only three or four seconds distant and somebody ordered 'Take cover!' Sub-Lieutenant Alan Clark, a helicopter observer, was on the bridge and looking in the direction of the Exocet; he saw an orange glow and a trace of smoke from the motor and also yelled, 'Take cover!' Then he threw himself down and put his arms over his head and face. Helicopter pilot Lieutenant Brian Leyshon saw the long, thin, finned missile and for the few seconds remaining he stared at it, unable to move.

The Exocet came in at six feet above water level and hit the centre of the ship, tearing a hole fifteen foot long by four foot, and knocking out all mechanical, weaponry and detection systems. Surgeon Lieutenant David Ward had been sitting in the sick bay reading when the explosion occurred – and the blast tore the door from its hinges. As the ship filled with black, acrid smoke he set about treating the injured. Burns were his main problem; one sailor had sixty per cent burns. The choking smoke beat back most of those who tried to get into the damaged area to rescue comrades but A.B. David Glasbey, after helping to rescue a badly burned man from below decks, went into a smoke-filled compartment with another sailor, to get some fire-fighting equipment. Both men were overcome by smoke; Glasbey was found and dragged out by Petty Officer Medical Assistant Jed Meager, wearing breathing apparatus, but the second man died.

The attempt at rescue was the result of training and instinct but the men in the area which had been directly hit would have died instantly.

The deck became unbearably hot, even white hot in places. The pumping system had been destroyed so hoses could not be used on the fire which roared through the central section. Two frigates, H.M.S. *Arrow* and H.M.S. *Yarmouth,* went alongside to help fight the fire, and helicopters brought fire-fighting equipment from elsewhere in the fleet. The *Sheffield*'s crew even lowered buckets into the sea and fought the blaze but the struggle was having no effect. Many found safety on the frigates though the *Yarmouth* had to detach on a submarine alert; an enemy submarine may have fired two torpedoes at *Sheffield* as it lay inert. After four-and-a-half hours, with increasing likelihood that the fire would explode the ship's magazines and kill everybody, Captain Salt had no alternative but to abandon ship. The *Sheffield* did not sink and later the engineer officer was put aboard by helicopter to see if she could be salvaged; he saw that the task was hopeless and the ship was sunk by explosives.

Captain Salt was interviewed on H.M.S. *Hermes* by Brian Hanrahan of the B.B.C. within hours of his rescue and television viewers were able to see the face of an exhausted man still in a state of shock; he was very much in control of himself but his efforts to remain so were apparent. 'Morale was at incredibly high level,' he said, 'the positive side to the *Sheffield* having been at sea since 17 November 1981. The team work was excellent and everybody showed immense calm and commonsense. Every captain would say that his ship's company is the best afloat but I am sure that mine is.' Much of what Salt said during the long interview showed that he could not accept the death of his ship, the first of several to be lost.

An improved weapon protection system might have saved the *Sheffield* and a different design as well as different materials in the building might well have reduced the fire and smoke danger.

'This is indeed a wonderful victory for French electronic know-how,' said a spokesman for the Avions Marcel Dassault company, which makes Exocet. He was more concerned about the reasons why the second missile did not hit the target than for the men who died.

The task force then had only two Type 22 destroyers, *Brilliant* and *Broadsword*, equipped with Sea Wolf missiles which can shoot down the Exocet missile.

Mrs Thatcher heard of the loss of the *Sheffield* while chairing a cabinet meeting and was shocked; her first reaction was concern for the victims' families. Even the Navy chiefs, realistic men, were 'totally stunned' by the devastating single blow which had destroyed the *Sheffield*. Yet the ship, commissioned in 1975, at a cost of £23.2 million, was well armed with a Lynx Mark II helicopter, twenty-two Sea Dart surface-to-air missiles, Sea Skua missiles for use against the lightly armoured ships and patrol boats and forty-four air-to-surface torpedoes for its helicopter to strike at enemy ships.

Naval experts all over the world were not slow to realise that the *Sheffield* had been vulnerable because she was operating outside her usual NATO waters, where ships can expect warning of enemy aircraft from their own air cover.

The British public, though horrified, still gave the Government strong support, despite Labour warnings that more lives would be lost. Support from abroad after the sinking of the *Belgrano* was less strong; the Irish government announced that it was appalled by 'the outbreak of what amounts to open war' and the Defence Minister, Mr Patrick Mower, said that 'obviously, the British are very much the aggressors now'. The sinking of the *Sheffield* did much to satisfy Mr Mower; in his view the Argentinians deserved their revenge.

In world opinion the destruction of H.M.S. *Sheffield* had the effect of producing a balance of shock. The West German government announced that it was 'dismayed' by the escalation of fighting and Paris was in a state of 'consternation'. Nevertheless, Britain kept the support of her allies at a meeting of NATO foreign ministers. At home, it was announced that two Sea Harriers had been lost by accident in dreadful weather conditions, so that until reserves arrived, the fleet had only seventeen aircraft. These reserves were on their way aboard Cunard's long container ship, *Atlantic Conveyor*, 15,000 tons, together with heavy duty Chinook and Wessex helicopters. She was one of a unique armada of fifty merchant ships with a total tonnage of 700,000 tons, operating a logistics chain to the Falklands area.

There was a minor British triumph on 9 May when a party of sixteen soldiers spectacularly boarded the Argentinian trawler *Narwal* by sliding down ropes from a helicopter. The trawler, earlier attacked by Harrier jets, was believed to be spying on the task force. On the same day a frigate bravely nosed along Falkland Sound, the strait separating East and West Falkland, probing bays and inlets for signs of enemy activity. A Lynx helicopter was sent up and machine-guns and a flare fired in the hope of drawing a response. Two nights later H.M.S. *Alacrity*, on patrol in the Sound, picked up on radar what turned out to be an Argentine fuel tanker in Grantham Sound. After *Alacrity* opened fire there was a huge and vivid explosion. With 1,500 troops on West Falkland it was important to cut them off from the base at Port Stanley and from supplies of any kind.

It was already clear to Fleet Headquarters planning staff at H.M.S. *Warrior* at Northwood, London, and to Major General Jeremy Moore of the Royal Marines who would command the land forces, that more men were needed. And they were soon on their way. The *Queen Elizabeth 2*, 67,000 tons, the world's second largest ship, was requisitioned to carry 5th Infantry Brigade and support units, 3,250 men in all, to the South Atlantic. The *QE2* was uniquely suitable to carry a large number of troops; it could make the 8,000 mile journey in ten days at a speed of 28.5 knots – fast enough to get away from any diesel-powered submarine. It would still be vulnerable to an air-to-surface missile attack but the chances of an Argentine plane flying within range of the ship were considered remote. The great danger was the *Santiago*, a World War II submarine bought from the United States in 1971. With a range of 12,000 miles, the 2,400 ton submarine could strike at the big British ships even deep into the Atlantic.

Conversion of the *QE2* was another remarkably efficient and rapid operation; in round-the-clock work helicopter pads were installed, military equipment was loaded and the ship changed from an expensive cruise liner into a trooper. Onto her marched 5th Brigade – made up of the Welsh Guards, the Scots Guards and the 7th Gurkhas – commanded by Brigadier Tony Wilson. Until a few weeks before, 5th Brigade had comprised the 2nd and 3rd Battalions the Parachute regiment, with the Gurkhas. The 3rd Battalion had sailed in *Canberra* and the 2nd in the ferry *Norland*. The two parachute units were immediately replaced by 2nd Battalion Scots Guards (Lieutenant-Colonel Mike Scott) and 1st Battalion Welsh Guards (Lieutenant-Colonel John Ricketts).

The Queen's personal assent in writing had to be obtained for the use abroad of the two Guards battalions. This is because the Household Division, which embraces her five regiments of Foot as well as her two regiments of Household Cavalry, are all her personal soldiers.

Captain Peter Jackson, Senior Master of the Cunard Fleet, had reassumed command of the *QE2* for its voyage to the South Atlantic; the ship's Relief

Master, Captain Alexander Hutcheson, was to be staff captain.

The ship's departure on 12 May was another extraordinary occasion, a display of mingled sorrow and pride and patriotism. The Welsh Guards boarded after dawn, marching in twos to the regimental band as it played *Men of Harlech*. They might have been off to the Sudan a century earlier. After the Welsh came the Scots Guards marching behind their piper with his pipes wailing *Scotland the Brave*. They brought with them their battle honours from Waterloo to Normandy and people wondered how 'The Falkland Islands' would look stitched in silver braid at the bottom of the regimental flag. A Scots sergeant said, 'Whatever happens down south, this is better than going to Northern Ireland.'

Last came the Gurkhas, under Lieutenant-Colonel David Morgan, tough, solid and disciplined, each with his kukri sheathed at his side. Their holy man came with them, furled umbrella over his arm.

The Defence Minister arrived early and a little later General Sir Edward Bramall, the Army's G.O.C. 5th Brigade was getting a send-off that only needed the Queen herself to make it perfect. Most of the families of the 3,000 men on board were bussed to the dock by the Army and they packed the quayside. It was the occasion which made famous Mrs Dawn Leyman of Swansea; she took off her bra and blouse and exposed herself to her husband, Lance Corporal Peter Leyman, and several hundred other soldiers. The garment was then delivered by dockside crane to Lance Corporal Leyman.

While the more open and obvious episodes of war – the sinking of ships and the shooting down of aircraft – were taking place the British were engaged in covert preparations for the inevitable landings. Highly trained men of the Special Air Service Regiment (S.A.S.) and Special Boat Service (S.B.S.) had been ashore in the Falklands from as early as 18 April. Before the British invasion of liberation about 300 of them were operating in small groups.

The S.A.S. had been public knowledge for many years and some of its actions – such as release of the hostages taken during the Iranian Embassy seige in London – were famous. But for many British people the existence of the S.B.S. came as a surprise, although its history also goes back to World War II. The marines who make up the S.B.S. like to think they are even tougher than the S.A.S. Toughness and physical hardihood was certainly necessary on the bleak Falklands when conventional protection from the weather could not be used. A four-man half-section spread a polythene sheet across a dip in the land and 'lay-up' in that. Occasionally they would make tea with a chemical cooker and during the day they huddled together for warmth.

The S.B.S. men started their mission at nightfall. Their primary task was reconnaissance, measuring the gradient of possible landing beaches, testing the sand to see what weight it would bear, counting and fixing on maps the position of Argentine outposts and guns. They travelled light on the Falklands, carrying little more than a folding-stock Armalite rifle, thirty pounds of explosives and a briefcase size radio which can send large amounts of information in a single brief electronic bleep – to be decoded in the radio room of a ship standing offshore. Around their belts the S.B.S. commandos carried a water bottle, a hunting/fighting knife, a handgun, snares, a fishing line and a food pouch. Everything else is in the small pack – food, spare socks, a waterproof poncho.

While the S.B.S. men nearly all came ashore in canoes or small boats, some of the S.A.S. men arrived by what they call H.A.L.O. – high altitude-low opening parachuting from a Hercules. They like to drop into the cover of deep valleys before opening their parachutes but there was little opportunity for that in the Falklands campaign.

Neither S.A.S nor S.B.S. arrived in the Gemini rubber boat found on a deserted beach together with a lifejacket bearing the name *Hermes*, and displayed by the Argentinians. The special forces prefer to use collapsible canoes which can be folded up and put in rucksacks. The S.B.S. do not paint the names of ships on their gear and the type of lifejacket has been replaced by a newer version. The only marine contingent still using the old lifejacket was the one stationed at Port Stanley. The boat and lifejacket were probably left on the beach by the marines who lost the battle when the Argentinians invaded.

Another task of both S.A.S. and S.B.S. was to locate the living places of the Falkland islanders, so that artillery and aircraft would avoid firing at them. An exacting assignment was to count the number of vehicles of all kinds and to note where they obtained their petrol. Fuel depots, ammunition dumps and stores would sooner or later become targets for air, naval or ground action.

The special services units were not, basically, sent onto the islands to kill the enemy – except in a planned raid. The object was to avoid contact and keep their presence secret. But on several occasions chance encounters occurred – and Argentine soldiers disappeared. Their bodies were carefully buried so that no search party could find them. The apprehension caused by their disappearance among their comrades was acute.

The S.A.S. and S.B.S. men had to avoid the human temptation to shelter in the homes of friendly islanders; there was no way of knowing how discreet any islander might be. Even a lonely abandoned hut could only be used if it had a sheltered way of withdrawal and a sentry on duty the whole time.

The S.A.S. and S.B.S. patrols were able to report that the islanders seemed well fed and in no apparent danger. They were slaughtering sheep, eating homegrown vegetables and many, having left Port Stanley, were settling in to sheep farms in the 'Camp', the name by which the Falklanders call the countryside. One patrol reported that the Argentinians appeared to be detaining up to a dozen people in a type of internment camp at Fox Bay, East Falkland. Among them was Dr Michael Haines, the island's chief medical officer and Stewart Wallace, a former member of the Falkland Islands Council, though the S.A.S. men did not know the names of the prisoners.

It was virtually certain that a resistance

underground would develop and that certain islanders would be suspect. Their detention was the work of Major Pablo Dowling, an Army officer of British extraction, in charge of Intelligence and the military police who imposed martial law. One of three Argentine officers of British stock with the invasion forces, Dowling threatened an eighteen-year-old dockyard worker with shooting for being found in the docks area.

A priority task for the special units was to know the position of every Argentinian aeroplane. This and all the other information was passed at intervals to a monitoring helicopter or to a ship offshore.

All of it finished up in the hands of Brigadier Julian Thompson of the Royal Marines, whose job it was to advise Admiral Woodward on the counter-invasion, when it came. A physically tough and highly intelligent officer of forty-seven, Thompson was to be the senior land officer until the arrival of Major General Moore. It was not yet possible to make a landing; the Government was still trying desperately to get the Argentinians out of the Falklands by diplomacy and the *threat* of overwhelming force. In the meantime Brigadier Thompson could use his special units more aggressively.

It is sobering to reflect that even at this critical time the British were making concession after concession in one attempt after another to reach a negotiated settlement. The Argentinian response was always the same – they would not obey U.N. Resolution 502, they would not take their occupation force from the Falklands and they would not negotiate sovereignty.

6 Raid on Pebble Island:
The Logistics Line

Steadily the momentum of war was overtaking the procrastination of negotiations. There was a limit to the amount of aerial bombing, naval bombardment and air combat that could be undertaken without ground action taking place. Woodward and Thompson had a large number of highly trained, keyed-up and expectant soldiers aboard the heaving ships and military logic demanded that they be used, even if only to show the enemy that they were as vulnerable to land action as to air and sea attack. The recapture of South Georgia, welcome though it had been, had not really hurt the Argentinians. A spirited, noisy and successful attack was needed.

Thompson knew from S.B.S. reports that the Argentinians had several military aircraft on the grass air strip of Pebble Island (Borbon Island to the Argentinians) on the north side of West Falkland. Most of the planes were twin-engined Pucaras, specially designed for attacking infantry with their 20mm Hispano Suiza cannons and bombs. Should the British land on East Falkland these aircraft could attack the landing troops from the rear, so their destruction was a priority. Also at the Pebble Island base were piles of ammunition and fuel and on First

Mountain, a peak of 900 foot behind the settlement, was a radar station, another prime target.

Thompson, with Admiral Woodward's approval, chose Pebble Island for Britain's demonstration of resolve and professional military skill and he chose the S.A.S. Regiment (not Marines as reported by all newspapers at the time) to make the attack, on the basis that they were skilled in the art of raiding and they would terrify the Argentinians more than any other unit would.

The episode was like something lifted from the commando history of World War II and super-imposed on the missile war.

The operation really began on the night of 11 May when eight men with canoes were landed on the West Falkland mainland south of Pebble Island. They were to reconnoitre the island and mark out places for the main party which would come in by helicopter. The seas were too rough for the advance party to cross until 13 May. They established observation posts and on the night of 14 May they marked the landing zones. By the early hours of 15 May a screaming gale was blowing, though it was a fairly clear night. The Argentinian garrison and the forty or so Falklanders who lived nearby, were asleep, apart from a few sentries who were not expected to be particularly alert. They would be sure that the weather was sufficient protection against an attack.

A single County class destroyer left the fleet in the darkness and headed for the slightly more sheltered waters of Elephant Bay. Meanwhile, aboard H.M.S. *Hermes*, the raiding party was ready to go: it comprised forty-eight S.A.S. men, in four-man teams, and a naval gunnery officer with a small team, including a radio operator, to spot for the ship's gun. They clambered into three Westland Commando Mark 22 helicopters – a specialised version of the Sea King – and took up their positions in the canvas seats. The helicopters were unshackled from the deck and took off for the short trip to the island, flying downwind; the noise of the engines was drowned by the force nine gale.

At the pre-arranged starting point for the raid, a few miles from the airstrip, the helicopters hovered a few feet above the ground and the S.A.S. men jumped out; the helicopters disappeared into the night almost immediately. The raiding party picked their way across the stony and sometimes boggy ground – just like parts of the Brecon Beacons where they had so often trained – while the artillery spotting team headed for higher ground and better observation. The timing of the raid depended on the gunner captain.

Having found a suitable spot he unpacked his laser rangefinder with its night sight and through it he saw the parked aircraft, the ammunition dump, the fuel store and the sentries. About a mile offshore the destroyer's 4.5 inch gun was ready to fire. The spotter gave the exact bearings of the first target, the gun opened up and the battle began. Brian Hanrahan, watching from the destroyer, said, 'The bulk of the island, black against the luminous sky, was suddenly lit by star shells and red tracer lines which climbed to the Argentine positions.'

After the star shells, to illuminate the ground for the S.A.S. men, came salvo after salvo of high explosive shells, the rate of fire designed as much to terrify as to destroy. The calm voice of the gunfire controller moved the gun just ahead of the S.A.S. men as they rapidly planted short-fuse explosives in the ammunition dump and fired tracer bullets into any loose boxes of ammunition – tracers contain phosphorous, which burns and quickly sets fire to whatever it hits.

Some teams of S.A.S. men sprinted down the runway to blow up some aircraft with explosives and others with phosphorous grenades. One by one the Pucaras blew up, as did a Skyvan, which the Argentinians used to ferry heavy equipment around the island. So, regretfully, did a few of the islanders' own light aircraft, which would inevitably have been used by the Argentinians.

The Argentinian troops were by now firing back, though at random as they had no clear target; when they called for assistance over their radio the destroyer jammed the signal. For a short time the S.A.S. men fired at the Argentinians and then called for a star shell so that they could fire at a gun which had come into action from the hill. The ship's gun also pounded this spot. Its shelling was so accurate that none of the one hundred rounds it fired that night fell near the civilian settlement, from where the islanders watched in excited satisfaction. The gunfire from this single ship was the heaviest British naval bombardment since World War II.

Then the spotting team and the S.A.S. men vanished into the night to rendezvous with the helicopters which quickly lifted them back to H.M.S. *Hermes* and the blacked-out destroyer ploughed through the heavy seas to rejoin the fleet. The first British land attack since the Argentinian occupation began had lasted thirty minutes and had been a complete success with eleven aircraft and the radar station destroyed, and fuel and ammunition dumps blown up. Only two S.A.S. men were slightly injured, having been concussed by mines belatedly detonated by the defenders.

In London the Defence Ministry, in announcing the attack, stressed that it has been a 'raid, not an invasion' to preempt the probable Argentinian assertion that the British had been repulsed.

The Ministry also announced that more raids could be expected; this information was designed to make the Argentinians more apprehensive and, more importantly, to delude them into believing that no full-scale counter invasion was imminent. Later that day Harriers made two bombing attacks on enemy positions at Port Stanley, as if designed to show that the British were indeed stepping up their various forms of raiding. These raids were from high altitude, the Harriers dropping 1,000 lb bombs fitted with airblast fuses to make them explode fifty feet above ground. Such bombs not only cause casualties but frighten enemy troops; experience has shown that soldiers are more terrified of airblast bombs than ground-exploding bombs, which often cause no casualties even when greatly damaging positions.

The British planners with the fleet had been advised by their controllers at operational head-quarters in Northwood that peace negotiations were reaching a critical stage. Admiral Woodward, convinced that his logistical flow was by now adequate to sustain any attack he might be ordered to make, was ready for the Government to switch from diplomacy to force. The problem of supply had been a worry at the back of the mind of all senior officers, army and navy, for two weeks. Invasions rarely succeed – or succeed only at great cost in lives – unless the momentum of supplies can be maintained, and enough provision has been made for contingencies.

Woodward now had 26,000 men in the South Atlantic and before long he would have one hundred ships. His warships needed refuelling every three days and his soldiers and sailors needed something like 600 tons of food and 1,500 tons of fresh water each week. Spares and ammunition had to be in abundance and, to allow for inevitable losses, he needed many more helicopters; without sufficient helicopters the invasion could not succeed.

But he could look back at a supply line which was functioning well. The chief elements of the task force conveyor belt comprised:

1: Twenty oil tankers, of which BP owned ten; two were Swedish under contract. With careful management the tankers ran a shuttle service, first between the fleet and Gibraltar and then Ascension Island, where supplies were being accumulated.

2: Five Hull trawlers, essential for intra-fleet work and for rescue and salvage of stricken warships or troopships.

3: Four other tugs with fire-fighting and salvage gear. They were the most powerful British tug, *Salvageman* 1,598 tons; *Irishman* and *Yorkshire*,

69

owned by United Towing; and a new and versatile tug, *Wimpey Seahorse* 1,599 tons, owned by Wimpey Marine.

4: Six chartered freighters, *Finnanger* (Norwegian) *Vinga Polaris, Lycson, Saxonia, Scottish Eagle* and the cold storage ship *Gaesport*, which also carried fruit.

5: Several container ships, principally *Atlantic Conveyor*, 15,000 tons, with deck strengthened for heavy duty Chinook and Wessex helicopters and her sister ship *Atlantic Causeway*, which carried the new 825 Squadron of Sea King helicopters and Wessex 5 Commando helicopters. Also there was the *Contender Bezant*, 11,000 tons, loaded with aircraft spares.

6: The cableship *Iris*, 3,873 tons, owned by British Telecom; this versatile ship carried satellite precision navigation equipment, multiple radio communications and a helipad. The fleet used *Iris* as a despatch vessel and inter-ship stores transport.

7: *Stena Seaspread*, 6,061-ton oil rig maintenance ship, with extensive workshops, fire-fighting equipment and diving chambers.

8: In addition Woodward could depend on several Royal Fleet auxiliary ships, including three survey ships converted to casualty ferries to get wounded to the hospital ships, eight tankers and three munitions and stores carriers.

Other merchant ships took stores as far as Ascension Island where the front-line vessels, working a shuttle service, collected them for the trips to the Falklands, 3,340 miles away or to South

Georgia, 3,820 miles distant. All the ships were vulnerable, at one point or another, to enemy attack. The Argentinians had one Guppy class submarine which could reach a point just north of Ascension Island, two Salta class submarines which could attack up to 1,000 miles south of Ascension and the land-based fighter-bombers which could reach targets anywhere around the Falklands themselves.

The key to the conveyor chain was Ascension Island. The volcanic island, seven miles long by five miles wide, had a population of fewer than 1,000 before the Falklands crisis – 500 St Helenians, 200 Americans, 160 Britons and a few South Africans. It was supplied from Britain every two months by sea and had five charter flights a year to rotate the staff working on the communications stations. Within a few weeks of the crisis the airport was recording as many as 350 take-offs and landings in a day.

The big ships on the way south used the large fleet anchorage as a stopover and men of the Parachute Regiment aboard *Canberra*, and of other units, went ashore to exercise. To accommodate military personnel tented camps sprang up and empty buildings, some built by Royal Marines in the nineteenth century, were rapidly renovated. The Navy managed the endless flow of food, ammunition, spare parts and general spares for the warships, Royal fleet auxiliaries, and merchantmen, and it also organised mail deliveries. The Army alone sent 100,000 letters and parcels a day from its London clearing station.

The Royal Engineers installed a large water distillation plant and the Army's Royal Corps of

Transport set up a base to co-ordinate movement of men and materials. During the campaign 250 Hercules and VC 10 aircraft, supplemented by chartered Boeing and Belfast aircraft – flew in thousands of passengers and several thousand tons of freight. Some squadrons of Harriers which were supposed to reach the battle zone by ship instead flew from Ascension, being refuelled in the air from the giant air tankers beside which a Harrier seems puny. The United States also quietly stockpiled on the island fuel and other supplies which the British had asked for, including at one time, 110 Sidewinder missiles.

Continuity of supply was more than usually vital, for the British landing force would be violating the standard theory that an attacking army must be much stronger than that which is defending. Even if the attacking troops were among the best in the world, as they were, raw conscripts in prepared positions could inflict heavy casualties on them. The attackers could not afford to be handicapped by having to husband their ammunition or by shortage of helicopter transport. But even allowing for some losses among ships in the supply line Woodward and his officers were sure that they could sustain 8,000 troops ashore, and in constant action.

Within a week of the Pebble Island raid the Defence Ministry's new Spanish-speaking radio station, beamed through a powerful transmitter on Ascension Island, was telling the Argentine garrison of the raid. 'Radio Atlantico' described the episode in graphic detail and warned the troops of the fearsome reputation of the S.A.S. soldiers. The decision to broadcast to the Falklands was based on the assumption that soldiers with much time on their hands in a static position will always be listening to programmes in their own language; in fact, the men of the task force were listening to the Argentinians' 'Radio Liberty' in English. In the same broadcast as the Pebble Island raid the garrison was told about their president's assertion that he was prepared to lose 40,000 of his own men to hold the islands.

Perhaps, the announcer suggested to the soldiers, they really were ready to die but she thought it more likely that they would want to live. Just existing on the Falklands must be hard enough, in the cold and wet and without food getting through the British blockade.

Also on the military front, Radio Atlantico presented a talk about the deadliness of the British commandos' rifles, which 'can fire through thick walls'; troops were advised to hide in deep fox holes. They were also warned about the danger of a dread disease spread by sheep parasites; soldiers should watch for cysts appearing in several parts of the body. Domestic politics were presented in some detail; in particular, why was it that the navy left all the suffering to the army and air force? An Argentine prisoner told how he and others in British hands were enjoying decent meals for the first time in a month. Another complained of being given only six bullets for his rifle. Radio Atlantico produced a Falklander, Gerald Dickinson of Port San Carlos, who reported that Argentine soldiers had begged for bread and, even worse that two sixteen-year-olds had been executed for desertion. Islanders had found plastic bags containing the bodies of soldiers who had died of exposure, according to Dickinson.

Whatever the effect of this propaganda on the Argentinian soldiers on the islands it had no influence in Buenos Aires. The war had had from the beginning an important psychological dimension. One reason for the Argentinian Service chiefs' confidence was the feeling that the British did not take Argentina seriously enough as a military power. To the virility conscious Argentinians this was offensive. Defence Minister Amadeo Frugoli said that the British task force had come to the Falklands expecting to find 'half-naked Indians as enemies, armed with arrows'. A few newspapers in Britain may have given the impression that the Argentinians would quickly collapse when faced with a professional army but the British politicians and service chiefs had no such illusion. Still, that was the Argentinian perception. 'We are amazed that many countries have doubts about our technological prowess,' an Argentinian officer said. 'We have nuclear technology, we build turbine engines, armaments, fire-control gear, and we buy the best from whoever has it.'

To a large degree Argentina's grotesque economic difficulties had stemmed from buying the best and from maintaining armed services beyond its needs. Also, while Argentina had bought the best material – though in some cases it was only the best secondhand – its generals had profound difficulties in knowing how to use it. Argentina's armed forces had not fought a war for a century and the army's main activity had been against its own people on the orders of a series of dictators. A nation without wars might consider itself fortunate but its Services deteriorate on an endless diet of parades and manoeuvres. No tradition of leadership, in principle and practice, can develop and generals can learn only from observing other nations' conflicts.

When Argentina found itself at war with Britain it had in men and equipment a formidable armed force. The army had 90,000 men and 250,000 reservists, plus 42,000 in para-military forces such as the Gendarmerie. The army's combatant composition was: two armoured brigades, four infantry brigades, two mountain brigades, one airmobile brigade, ten artillery regiments.

The principal armoured vehicles were 100 M-4 Sherman medium tanks, 80 AMX-13 light tanks and an unknown number of TAM medium tanks, developed by the German firm Thyssen Henschel to an Argentinian requirement. The army was strong in artillery including 155mm and 105mm towed and self-propelled guns and many heavy mortars. In anti-aircraft defence the army depended on 20mm, 35mm, 90mm and 105mm guns.

The army relied on the model 68 recoilless rifle firing a 105mm shell to stop enemy tanks and against enemy armour it could also use the Oerlikon type of GDF-001 with its anti-aircraft mounting. The Argentinian armoured personnel carrier was the AMX-VC1, able to carry twelve infantrymen up a sixty per cent gradient. Some of these were taken to the Falklands. The army also had its own air service, mainly Puma and Bell helicopters and Pucara attack planes.

The standard infantry weapon was the PA3 9mm sub-machine gun. Made by the Fabrica Militar de Armas Portatilas at Rosario, the PA3 is a modern weapon exclusive to Argentina. Its limitation in the Falklands was its maximum effective range of 200 metres. In the open country of the Falklands many Argentinians were armed with the Belgian 7.62mm rifle, similar to the British LIAI 7.62m self-loading rifle with its range of 600 metres.

The Argentinian Navy, with 35,000 personnel, was a formidable force when the war began. The major warships were:

Name	Tonnage Type	Armament
Salta	1,300 German IK 68-type diesel submarine	Torpedoes
San Luis	1,300 German IK 68-type diesel submarine	Torpedoes
*Sante Fé	2,400 ex-US World War II diesel submarine	Torpedoes
Santiago Del Estero	2,500 ex-US World War II diesel submarine	Torpedoes
Vienticinco de Mayo	16,000 ex-British World War II carrier	Skyhawk, Sea King
*General Belgrano	11,000 ex-US pre-World War II cruiser	6-in and 5-in guns, Seacat
Hercules	3,200 British Type 42 destroyer	Exocet, Sea Dart, 4.5-in gun, Lynx

*Sunk

Santisima Trinidad	3.200 British Type 42 destroyer	Exocet, Sea Dart, 4.5-in gun, Lynx
Rosales	2,100 ex-US World War II destroyer	5-in and 3-in guns
Almirante Stormi	2,100 ex-US World War II destroyer	5-in and 3-in guns
Segui	2,200 ex-US World War II destroyer	Exocet, 5-in and 3-in guns
Hipolito Bouchard	2,200 ex-US World War II destroyer	Exocet, 5-in and 3-in guns
Piedra Buena	2,200 ex-US World War II destroyer	Exocet, 5-in and 3-in guns
Comodoro Py	2,400 ex-US World War II destroyer	Exocet, 5-in gun
Drummond	1,200 French Type A69 corvette	Exocet, 4-in gun
Guerrico	1,200 French Type A69 corvette	Exocet, 4-in gun
Granville	1.200 French Type A69 corvette	Exocet, 4-in gun

In addition the Navy had ten coastal minesweepers and at least fourteen landing craft. The Naval Air Service consisted of 3,000 men with seventy combat aircraft, including fifteen helicopters. The attached Marine force – known as the Naval Infantry Corps – had 6,500 men.

The Air Force had a total strength of 22,500. It had about 250 aircraft when the fighting began.

In addition it had more than 130 transport aircraft and about eighty helicopters. Many of the pilots and maintenance crews were trained in the United States and were considered to be the élite of the country's armed forces. Unlike the bulk of the army and navy the pilots were all volunteers and most were career officers.

The air force had problems beside those of British opposition, the most serious being mechanical ones. These came about from a four-year embargo on spare parts imposed by President Carter to punish Argentina for human rights violations. Pilots were complaining before the hostilities that ejection seats did not work, that there were many mechanical faults and that they were short of ammunition for the original Skyhawks. In addition, mechanics for the newer Mirages and Etendards were not as well trained as for the Skyhawks.

The Argentinian General Staff sent to the Falklands only two fully trained infantry units with armoured personnel carriers, a few light tanks and some anti-aircraft units. The rest of the occupation force was made up of relatively raw troops under training in the reserve. Still, stiffening by highly trained regular troops and national pride could make them formidable enough. The reason for not sending a larger number of troops may have been the anticipated difficulty of supplying them, though in the twenty-six days between the occupation and Britain's imposition of a total sea and air blockade much more material could have been taken into the islands.

A fundamental difference of military principle split Admiral Anaya and General Dozo. Anaya, though he was hawkish and talked in tough terms, was unwilling to take risks with his fleet. 'The Navy's first job is to protect the mainland,' he frequently explained. Dozo, in contrast, was willing to risk his pilots and planes; indeed he had no choice if the British were to be stopped. But the disproportionate burden carried by his air service angered him and caused friction within the Junta.

Anaya would probably have faced a ship-to-ship battle, he might even have pitted his carrier and aircraft against *Hermes* or *Invincible* but he greatly feared the British nuclear-powered submarines. The sinking of the *Belgrano* confirmed him in his fears; this incident will be seen as the key cause of the Argentine navy's refusal to face action. The sinking was, therefore, justified.

The contrast in logistics between Britain and Argentina was startling. Argentina was fighting the war on its own doorstep and should have had the advantage. Not having taken the British counter-threat seriously enough, the leaders were slow to build up their forces on the Falklands – they needed at least a division of 20,000 – and failed lamentably to supply them. The British, entirely without a land base and operating wholly from ships, had reacted quickly and despite enormous distances had a much better supply line than the Argentinians.

As yet another round of non-negotiations foundered in the third week of May the British War Cabinet reshaped the Falklands invasion strategy. Earlier it had decided on a careful step-by-step approach, a creeping invasion. Now the emphasis was on speed – for four reasons:

1: Continued deterioration in the weather.

2: Information that Argentina was receiving additional military equipment, notably surveillance aircraft with submarine detection devices and air-to-surface missiles from Brazil.

3: Strong advice from both the u.s. and France – and from certain private sources in Britain – to act quickly and decisively in combat.

4: The need to accomplish the invasion before the UN Security Council could consider a ceasefire resolution to the conflict; this would simply leave the 'burglar with his spoils', as Mrs Thatcher had put it.

On Thursday 20 May the House of Commons met for its sixth debate on the Falklands and Mrs Thatcher criticised Galtieri and his Junta colleagues for obduracy, delay, deception and bad faith in the peace negotiations. Britain had made eight sets of proposals and Argentina's rejection of the final proposals had implications of the utmost gravity. 'It's Britain who stands up for the international rule of law, and it's Britain who says, "Enough is enough, this must stop,"' the Prime Minister said, and she warned, 'Difficult days lie ahead.'

It is likely that as she spoke her order to the Chief of Defence Staff to invade was already being passed on.

In New York the Secretary General Peres de Cueller said with desperate pessimism, 'The patient is still alive but in intensive care.'

And in a television interview Dr Costa Mendez was saying that Argentina was ready to negotiate – but its troops would not leave the island and

Argentinian sovereignty had to be guaranteed in advance.

The patient was dead and Señor de Cueller knew it. Full scale war was inevitable.

7 The Liberation Invasion

The American Chiefs of Staff at the Pentagon in Washington suspected that a British landing was imminent because at 4 p.m. on Thursday 20 May Britain cut off the normal flow of intelligence data to the U.S. about the location of their own and Argentinian ships in the South Atlantic. Only after many hours were American intelligence experts able to pinpoint the exact site of the British landing. President Reagan was able to say, truthfully, that he knew of the invasion only after the attack began.

The exact site was Port San Carlos, in the Falkland Sound, which divides East and West Falkland. The S.A.S. and S.B.S. had reported that only about 120 Argentine troops were in the vicinity, more for observation than defence. From S.B.S. information Admiral Woodward knew that the anchorage was deep and photographs and maps showed it to be spacious enough to take several ships at the one time. Another advantage was that it was to a large extent protected from Exocet missiles, which need a reasonable amount of ocean space to be fully effective. From Brigadier Julian Thompson's more military requirements, Port San Carlos had a defensive perimeter of hills for a safe bridgehead and from here he could move in two and possibly three directions on Port Stanley. The disadvantage was purely naval – the destroyers and frigates had little room to manoeuvre if they came under air attack and would simply have to stay and fight it out; their job, after all, was to protect the supply ships, assault ships and the bridgehead during its vulnerable period of establishment. Much could be moved by helicopters from ships further out but heavy vehicles, missile launchers, bulldozers and large loads of ammunition were too heavy for them.

The Argentinians did not know exactly where the attack might come, as the Navy frequently shelled various possible landing points. This was not only to harass the defenders but to get them used to the idea that a shelling did not necessarily precede a landing.

An 'accident of war' had brought tragedy on Wednesday 19 May when a Sea King helicopter ferrying troops between vessels was struck from underneath by a rearing ship as the helicopter was taking off and fell into the water. Nine men were rescued but twenty-one were drowned; most were members of the S.A.S., though their parent regiment was listed on casualty returns. This loss during operations was a great blow to the small, tightly knit S.A.S. regiment which does so much and says so little.

Captains of ships told the men over the Tannoy on the night of 20 May, that the landing was on. On *Invincible* the announcement was made by Captain Tony Provost. 'As you know, there has been a meeting of the cabinet this morning and we have just had a signal saying that it has been decided that the landing will take place tomorrow morning.'

North-east of the Falklands the fleet divided. The

largest group of forty, led by the assault ships *Fearless* and *Intrepid*, each carrying 700 marines and paratroopers, and guarded by frigates and destroyers, headed west. With them went *Canberra* and a flotilla of supply ships. They steamed along the northern coast of East Falkland to Falkland Sound.

Hermes and *Invincible*, with their protective screen of frigates and destroyers, headed south past the entrance to Port Stanley to a point somewhere near Lively Island; as they moved the Sea Harriers took off to harass the enemy positions at Port Stanley, Goose Green and Fox Bay. The warships' guns also opened up, with particular concentration on Stanley, while two warships detached to bombard the Argentine positions at Port Louis. Raiding parties went ashore at all these positions and there was some hand-to-hand fighting. The diversions were designed to convince General Menendez and his staff that the main attack was to be on the south of the Falklands – and the stratagem worked.

While most of the warships stayed in the Sound itself the *Fearless* and *Intrepid*, followed by the *Canberra*, turned east between the peaks of Chancho Point and Fanning Head to the natural anchorage of four-mile estuary of the San Carlos River.

The importance of H.M.S. *Fearless*, fulfilling the role for which she had been commissioned in 1965, cannot be underestimated. With a capacity of 5,000 miles at a speed of twenty knots, *Fearless* was built on the principle of a catamaran. In the booms is living accommodation; between them is a dock which is flooded to launch four landing craft. Another four smaller landing craft are swung on davits, and she carries five helicopters and up to sixteen tanks and twenty-three trucks. Most important, the ship has a headquarters complete with communications centre from which a ground commander can control his attack.

At 4 a.m. men of the Royal Marines 40th, 42nd and 45th Commandos and 2nd and 3rd Parachute Battalions clambered over the side of their ships into the sixteen shallow landing craft, many with names of the Knights of the Round Table – *Sir Bedevere*, *Sir Galahad* and *Sir Geraint*, for instance. Michael Nicholson, I.T.N.'s correspondent, described the scene in his usual vivid manner: 'With black faces, heavily camouflaged, carrying enormous packs with mortars, rifles, machine-guns, anti-tank rockets – all this strapped to their backs – they clambered down the rope netting at the side of their mother ship into their landing craft. They were queueing up alongside the ships like taxis.'

At 6.30 a.m., with dawn only minutes away, a destroyer and two frigates led the landing craft into the landing beaches. On reaching the narrows the ships shelled the Argentinian observation posts on the heights, previously pinpointed by S.A.S. and S.B.S. patrols. Each landing craft had a precise beaching point whether in Fanning Harbour, Sand Bay, San Carlos settlement or Ajax Bay. They raced for the shore, grounded, lowered their ramps, and the troops splashed through the shallows. Soon the 29th Commando Regiment of the Royal Artillery followed with their 105mm howitzers and Rapier anti-aircraft missiles, then 59 Company of the Royal Engineers with explosives and bridging equipment, and a hundred men of 2nd Troop of the Blues and Royals cavalry, with sixteen Scimitar and Scorpion light tanks.

Nobody present at San Carlos was old enough to have witnessed the D-Day landings in Normandy in 1944 but the San Carlos episode was like Normandy in miniature, with the significant exception that San Carlos was virtually unopposed. Lieutenant Roberto Oscar Reyes of the 12th Argentine Infantry had forty-two men in positions near the civic hall in San Carlos but they quickly withdrew. As they ran onto the hills they brought down, with small arms fire, two Marine Gazelle observation helicopters, and the crews were killed.

On the ships thousands of anxious eyes strained through the lifting darkness and soon picked up the troops moving rapidly up the hills behind Port San Carlos; others were fanning out north and south while more landing craft were reaching the jetty of the port itself. In the midst of this military action islanders in their pyjamas and dressing gowns came out to greet the troops and offer cups of tea but some of San Carlos residents did not know of the counter-invasion until Royal Marines came to their homes. A sheep farmer told a *Daily Mail* reporter that he answered a knock on the door to find a Marine officer who said, 'Don't worry, I am a British marine. Stay indoors. You are quite safe. We are here now.' Some soldiers were already posing for photographs with the fifty or so civilians of San Carlos settlement. One photograph, showing Sergeant Major Laurie Ashbridge of 3rd Paras having a cup of tea with a group of happy

Falklanders, appeared in practically every British newspaper.

The well trained troops at once dug in and lines of trenches showed on the hillsides. In many places in the peaty bog the trenches and weapon pits soon had eighteen inches of water but they were safer than in the open should aircraft strafe the defences. The surrounding countryside seemed to change its entire appearance under the observers' eyes, becoming an instant army base. Within an hour twenty ships had anchored in Fanning Harbour which became a place of intense activity as vast amounts of food, fuel, trucks, ammunition, tents and pontoons were rushed ashore. In a flurry of co-ordinated activity stores of all kinds were carried above the waterline, piled and then redistributed. Helicopters took in one load after another, slung on ropes beneath them.

Brigadier Julian Thompson and his staff set up 3rd Commando Brigade H.Q. while the marines and paras quickly secured a perimeter. It was vital to make the bridgehead as strong as possible before the Argentinians launched their inevitable counter-attack.

Smaller Cymbeline radars were quickly in position to protect the troops aginst hit-and-run mortar attacks. When an enemy patrol was picked up on the Cymbeline screen it could be engaged by field artillery while armour would face not only artillery but mortars and Milan and Carl Gustav anti-tank rockets. Some of the infantry carried shoulder-fired Blowpipe missiles, with disposable launchers which were discarded once the missile had been fired.

As the landing force went in Harriers of 800 and 801 Fleet Air Arm squadrons were already lined up on the decks of the *Hermes* and *Invincible*, with their pilots strapped in, ready for the 'red alert' which would get them airborne within seconds. The first air attack came from the east, from the Port Stanley direction. Pucaras – described by the B.B.C. reporter Robert Fox as 'unpleasant guerrilla-warfare planes' – flew in so low they were upon the bridgehead almost before the British knew it. Some headed for the ships, others strafed the troops ashore. Because of the volume of fire sent up against them the Pucaras did little damage and if they were not quickly out of the way they were destroyed.

A more formidable threat then developed, as expected, from the West and sixteen Skyhawks and Mirages swooped in. Harriers from the *Hermes* and *Invincible* were quickly in the air to meet them and then the Argentinian pilots had to face the streaking missiles. Some bombs exploded harmlessly on the hillsides, others hit the water, as one wave of Skyhawks and Mirages succeeded another. Clearly they had orders to make the warships their main targets, though the *Canberra* and other ships were also attacked.

The Argentinians' main success was to bomb the frigate H.M.S. *Ardent*, the most exposed of the warships. Under her young commander, Captain Alan West, thirty-five, *Ardent* was one of the fleet's most modern ships. She was formidably armed with Exocet anti-ship missiles, Seacat anti-aircraft missiles and the standard 4.5 inch gun but her main job was to hunt submarines. Her crew fought hard and during the attack John Leake, a former soldier turned NAAFI manager, rushed from below deck to become a machine-gunner as the *Ardent* put up a last defiant stand under the rain of bombs and rockets. With cool commonsense he brought down a Skyhawk by firing a machine-gun straight upwards so that the aircraft flew through the bullets. Hit by 1,000 lb bombs and rockets, the *Ardent* was doomed and sank; twenty-four of her crew of 170 were killed and thirty injured. In Buenos Aires Navy lieutenant Owen Guillermo Crippa was credited with having sunk the *Ardent* from his Aeromacchi jet. Hit by a rocket, he had to eject but was rescued.

Two Skyhawk 1,000 lb bombs five feet long smashed through H.M.S. *Antrim* and wedged in the machinery. Bomb disposal experts were taken by helicopter to the ship and the steam and gas powered turbine engines were switched off while the two men, an officer and N.C.O., crawled through the maze of pipes. Meanwhile the crew of thirty-three officers and 238 men were moved to the ends of the ship, though the gunners stayed at their posts. The bomb disposal men had sophisticated cutting equipment and brass spanners which produce no sparks, among other special items, but the position of the bombs made their handling difficult. In the dark, steamy atmosphere defusing the bombs required much patience, immense concentration and great skill but after several hours the pair came on deck to say that the bombs could now be safely manhandled up from below and thrown overboard.

As night fell on 21 May the British had a bridgehead of ten square miles, a safe enough area to consider themselves re-established on the Falklands. Amid all the hectic activity of the day and all the words spoken and written about it one comment stands out. It came from a farmer who answered a knock on his door and found a soldier there. 'It's about time,' the farmer said.

When darkness brought an end to the fighting the Argentinians, after forty separate attacks, had lost nine Mirages, five Skyhawks, two Pucaras and four helicopters. Eight of the enemy planes were destroyed by Harriers.

Ashore thousands of men were in foxholes dug at least four feet deep or more into stone and clay or in peat. From ground level the hillsides looked mole-infested; from the air relatively little could be seen because of the way the trenches and holes were camouflaged. The liberation army had settled in, though to a dark nightlife for there was already a strict order forbidding any form of light for the sixteen hours of darkness.

That evening a message from Admiral Sir John Fieldhouse, Commander-in-Chief Fleet, was sent to all units. 'You did well. They will not be so keen to come on now.' The Argentinian pilots might not have been keen but come on they did – though not at once.

The invasion had been a calculated military risk of classic proportions. The 4,500 troops put ashore had only enough fuel, food and ammunition for a certain four days and at most a worrying six days. It was not possible that first day to land the heavy equipment the troops needed to continue an advance. Had the supply line been cut the following day, Saturday, the whole assault could have withered. Astonishingly, the Argentinians gave the British bridgehead thirty-six hours peace, apart from a hesitant raid by two Skyhawks which turned and fled when Harriers raced to meet them. The Argentine Air Force spent the day resting and regrouping – a delay which demonstrated lack of command experience.

On Saturday night, 22 May, a destroyer intercepted the *Monsunen*, a Falkland Islands Company vessel which the Argentinians had commandeered to ferry troops, stores and ammunition around the islands. After being illuminated with star shells the vessel ran aground and was abandoned by her crew, the loss of its supplies was a blow to the Argentinians. Islanders later recovered the ship.

The Argentine aircraft returned to the fight on Sunday 23 May and in the afternoon H.M.S. *Antelope*, 2,500 tons (Commander Nicholas Tobin) was hit by bombs. The attacking Skyhawk flew so low over the *Antelope* that its belly scraped the frigate's radar antenna. Michael Nicholson, watching the attack, said that immediately after dropping its bombs a missile blew the plane to pieces. One bomb started a fire, the other did not explode. Staff Sergeant Jim Prescott, Royal Engineers, was helicoptered aboard to deal with it. As he drew the fuse the bomb blew up. The gallant Jim Prescott died and some of the crew were wounded as a huge fireball rose from the blazing ship. The fire became uncontrollable and she was abandoned. Helicopters were at once on the scene picking up survivors while landing craft went alongside to lift off any remaining crew. Brian Hanrahan, of the B.B.C., who watched the operation described it as 'a courageous and orderly rescue against the ever present danger of further explosions'.

It was to be expected that the Galtieri Junta would order a major air attack on 25 May, Argentina's national day. Expectation became reality as waves of Mirages and Skyhawks came in low over the hills of West Falkland and from the south up Falkland Sound. In fierce air battles over the task force the Argentine Air Force again paid a high price, as one pilot after another was shot down by Harriers or by missiles from the ships. Some broke through the Harrier screen; in one incursion four Skyhawks screeched over the bay, one to be hit and 'splashed', another to be damaged. The others fled.

During the first week after the landing the daring of the Argentinian pilots almost reached the desperation of the Japanese kamikaze pilots who deliberately flew their bomb-laden aircraft into American warships during the Pacific campaign of World War II. Nigel Nicholson said, 'On our ship alone eighteen guns are putting out 24,000 rounds of ammunition. Imagine what it must feel like for a pilot in a Mirage or Skyhawk suddenly seeing this wall of lead. There is no escape from it ... Those pilots who come into our defences hugging the water, as they did today, coming along the line of the river to get into us before we can detect them – they have been daring, they have been courageous.'

H.M.S. *Coventry* (Captain David Hart-Dyke) was on picket duty north of Falkland Sound, protecting the support vessels landing supplies and equipment at San Carlos. First she was approached by a reconnaissance aircraft which *Coventry*'s gunners shot down with a Sea Dart but not before the pilot had radioed *Coventry*'s position to his base.

Four Skyhawks were sent against the destroyer, one to be downed by a Sea Dart from the ship, the others by Rapier missiles from the bridgehead. Some hours later six more Skyhawks attacked the *Coventry*, flying very low from the direction of Pebble Island, and this time her gunners' skill could not save her. Bombs hit her and she capsized; nineteen of the crew of 280 died and another twenty were injured. H.M.S. *Broadsword*, which was with the *Coventry*, was also attacked and damaged but remained in action, as did H.M.S. *Argonaut*, hit earlier.

The *Coventry* had only one Sea Dart launcher; it reloaded rapidly but the radar system could not switch to a new target until the first one had been destroyed and disappeared from the screen. With several planes attacking the ship simultaneously one was bound to get through. The Argentinian pilots radioed to their base at Rio Gallegos that the picket ship was out of action. The Super Etendards were then sent off with two of Argentina's very thin reserve of Exocets – there was probably only one left at this time – hoping to bag an aircraft carrier or the *Canberra*. Refuelled in mid-air, they were able to fly much further east than the British expected, so that they approached from the rear, where their radar picked up a large blip; it was the big *Atlantic Conveyor* making for Port San Carlos with some priceless cargo of giant Chinook helicopters and fuel. Both Etendards fired their Exocets and one hit the large ship, killing twelve of the crew, including the captain. The Ministry of Defence announced that the helicopters had already been 'reallocated'; some had but most were still on *Atlantic Conveyor* and many were destroyed by fire. The Ministry later said that the ship had not sunk and that valuable material had been salvaged. This was justifiable disinformation but in fact the ship did sink and its loss was a sharp blow. Harriers had been using *Atlantic Conveyor* as a third aircraft carrier, with the result that Admiral Woodward could disperse his Harriers with greater safety.

The decision to abandon ship was taken by Captain Michael Layard, the naval officer in tactical command of the ship. Through discipline and training a hundred men of the three services and thirty-four Merchant Marine seamen survived the sinking and explosion. Helicopters plucked them from the stricken *Atlantic Conveyor* itself or from life rafts. The loss of Captain Ian North, the last man from the ship, was a blow to his native city of Liverpool. He had become famous as 'Captain Birdseye' because of his similarity to the bearded captain of the television advertisement.

On the night of 25 May, a bad day for the British forces, Defence Secretary John Nott broadcast to the Falkland Islanders through the BBC World Service programme *Calling the Falklands*. 'Be of good cheer,' he said, 'for you can now look forward to the early prospect of liberation and a return to your normal way of life.' At the same time the Argentine High Command, carried away with its own rhetoric and propaganda, was claiming that the British invaders were dying without ammunition, water or medical assistance. In fact, the frontline surgical teams, who had been among the first ashore, were relieved to have so little work to do.

The Argentine fliers had a whole-hearted respect for their British adversaries while they themselves were given, by their own people, the heroic title of *pingos del aire* – horses of the air. They evolved a language of their own, so that a 'fatty' was a British warship and a 'phantom' an enemy aircraft. Getting out of the way of a British missile was described as a new dance step, the 'Misilera'.

The skill of the Argentinian pilots was not surprising; many had been trained in Israel by the world's most experienced combat fliers. The training was superb but few of the pilots had practised attacking over water and none had faced real missiles which locked on and could rarely be evaded.

Mirage aircraft are normally well equipped with air-to-air weapons such as the French R530 or Sidewinder heat-seeking missiles with which to shoot down opposing fighters, but there is little evidence that the Argentine fighter pilots ever set out with the intention of taking on the Sea Harriers, whose pilots they feared. In the short time they could spend in the operational area they had been told to find and strike a ship, preferably a warship – nothing else mattered, not even their own safety.

Flying out from the mainland at high level to conserve fuel, the pilots knew that they would be spotted and reported to the Sea Harriers by radar picket ships. Using cloud for concealment, the attackers then descended rapidly to sea level and even flying through sea spray, swinging in around Foul Island to the Falkland Sound to find the ships.

Without effective ground radar to guide them in – the radar posts had been demolished by S.A.S. attacks – the Mirage pilots were at a great disadvantage. Those that escaped the Harrier cordon had then to run the gauntlet of Sea Dart, Sea Wolf and Rapier missile defences. No aircraft could loiter in the battle area to look for a target for it would quickly be caught by Rapier or Blowpipe.

Their fuel gauges would then be half empty but the pilots had to climb back to high altitude to be able to reach their mainland base. It was known that several aircraft crashed on returning through fuselage or engine damage and a few went into the sea when they ran out of petrol.

On Monday 24, in the third big air-sea battle in four days, seven Argentine planes were shot down by Sea Harriers, naval gunfire and missiles launched from the San Carlos bridgehead. A Harrier crashed after take-off, killing its pilot. In one air battle two Sea Harriers took on three faster Mirages over Pebble Island; the leading Harrier hit the first two Mirages with Sidewinder missiles, the first confirmed double kill by a British pilot in the Falkland dogfights. His wingman hit the third Argentine Mirage. Two pilots were seen to eject.

By 28 May, a week after the landing, the Argentinians had lost sixty aircraft and almost as many pilots; almost certainly it had no planes left in the islands other than a few helicopters and Pucaras. Further sorties from the mainland were inevitable but the Argentine Air Force no longer had the capability to sustain major low-level attacks.

The British success at San Carlos was evident from

the vehement demands by a dozen Latin American nations to address the UN Security Council; they wanted to denounce the British 'aggression'. Even Dr Costa Mendez was protesting against this aggression – and at the same time he was saying that the British attacks had been repulsed. This was a change of attitude; even by the night of the 23 May he was denying that a landing had taken place.

There was some hope, in Britain, the United States and Europe, that an all-out battle for the Falklands might not be necessary, even though Intelligence reports assessed General Menendez as a diehard leader from a proud military family who would keep his troops in position even if he had to shoot some as an example. And some of his officers did indeed shoot their own men.

That week Mrs Thatcher had said that the British servicemen in the Falklands were 'the most marvellous fighting forces in the world. They are courageous, dedicated and fighting for a just cause.'

She had seen evidence of the courage of her airmen and sailors. Soon her soldiers would show this Iron Lady what metal they were made of.

8 'Advance to Contact': Goose Green

With the bridgehead made secure, largely by naval sacrifice, the responsibility for taking the enemy positions passed to the army. Bombardment from the sea and air could cause great damage, inflict casualties and depress morale but only the foot soldiers could capture and hold positions, take prisoners and force a surrender. The decisions now to be taken would be made by Brigadier Thompson until the arrival of Major General Moore, who up to this point had necessarily been more concerned with overall management of his land forces – supply and flow of weapons, ammunition and transport, position of reinforcements – than with direction in the field.

It is easy to draw parallels between Margaret Thatcher and Winston Churchill, but there was one big difference. Churchill often interfered with the way his generals conducted battles and sometimes urged battles and campaigns which the generals knew could be disastrous. Mrs Thatcher at no time tried to be the commander at sea or in the field and she saw to it that her Defence Secretary kept out of tactical decision-making. She said many times that the timing of attacks must be left to the commander of the task force or to the commander land forces. The only restraints placed on the commanders were that casualties be kept to a minimum, that there be no bombing of the Argentine mainland airbases and that the invasion itself – though not its tactical timing – should be a matter of political decision. Many servicemen were critical of the decision not to bomb the mainland airfields from which they suffered so much harassment but such bombing was neither operationally practicable nor politically desirable.

With ground rather than a heaving ship under their feet, the paras and marine commandos quickly regained some of the confidence they had lost aboard ship. A soldier is accustomed to *ground* and the trained fighting man uses it, constantly assessing the terrain he is looking at for the cover it might afford him from view and from enemy fire. He learns to recognise the ground which may be mostly easily dug for trenches and that which will be stony and unyielding. He sees at once lines of possible advance and makes sure that, where possible, he has a line of retreat for an emergency. The soldiers who had been with the fleet for so long in the stormy South Atlantic were relieved to be back on an element they understood.

Before any general advance from San Carlos, about forty men of the S.A.S. in three groups carried out harassing attacks towards Darwin and Goose Green. They were ordered not to engage the enemy at close quarters but to make as much noise as possible. To do this they had to carry a great weight of mortar and machine-gun ammunition, about eighty pounds each, in their exhausting twenty-hour non-stop foray. It was learned later that the Argentinian commander at Goose Green reported that his position was under attack by an entire battalion.

After this operation the S.A.S. shot down a Pucara with a Blowpipe missile and possibly damaged another. The men who went on this raid did so in the knowledge that eighteen of their comrades had been killed in the helicopter crash shortly before.

The service censors habitually deleted reference to S.A.S. and S.B.S. activities and as neither unit ever mentions its heroic achievements it is only through indirect inquiry that correspondents and historians can give them some of the credit they deserve. Two squadrons, about 200 men, served in the Falklands: nineteen were killed and five wounded. It may be said here that the S.A.S. did not have seven men taken prisoner in Argentina, despite claims by the C.I.A., published in some London papers.

While the special units were engaged on patrolling and reconnaissance work, the men within the San Carlos perimeter worked themselves to a standstill to accumulate, disperse and camouflage stores and equipment. Vast amounts were needed; just one 105mm gun could fire ten tons of shells in a single bombardment. This labour was punctuated by enemy air raids, sometimes directed against the troops rather than at the ships. In one attack four marines were killed and twenty wounded by a direct hit. As a raid came in the warning would go out, 'Air raid red, air raid red, take cover now!' Then the ever-ready missile crews would go into action, their rockets whooshing away from the launchers, mostly to follow their target relentlessly and hit.

In one respect life on board ship had been better than on the land – the food was more varied. Ashore the troops depended on the 'Arctic pack', described on the cardboard box which held it as '24-hour ration pack Arctic (one man)'. Four menus were available. The breakfast was the same in all four, porridge and drinking chocolate. The meal differed in choice between ham, chicken, ham *and* chicken and bacon spreads for plain biscuits, to go with fruit and chocolate biscuits, chocolate caramels, nuts and raisins and dextrose sweets. The main meal, all dehydrated, offered a choice of three soups, beef, curried beef, mutton or chicken supreme granules, rice or mashed potato powder; apple or apricot flakes completed the meal. All the soldier had to do was add water and heat his meal with his naphtholene stove. Officers and men carried two Arctic packs and were resupplied every two days.

Easy to carry and easy to prepare, the food had all that was required to provide a fighting man with the calories needed to keep him fit and as energetic as possible. Where soldiers were within reach of the ships the crews took them vast quantities of freshly baked rolls, a luxury on a battlefield where it is difficult for mobile field kitchens to operate. Soldiers lucky enough to be near Falkland homes were given mutton broth, which was eagerly accepted. The sheep's brains fritters, an island specialty, were not popular.

Argentinian soldiers in the trenches were given a CF ration – C for combat, F for supplementary. The food was hermetically sealed in a tin weighing five pounds and containing twenty items, based on meat and macaroni, chocolate, instant cocoa, vitamin C tablets, powdered fruit juice and biscuits. Other things included a small aluminium stove, solid fuel, matches, a plastic bottle of water, toilet paper, stationery, envelopes and religious articles. The kit also contained a message to the soldier: 'We, the men and women who packed this ration, volunteers of all ages, are your brothers in this struggle for justice, until final victory. Long live the Fatherland.' Nevertheless, the Argentinians were often hungry because ration packs were in short supply.

From Port San Carlos onwards the terrain itself, as well as the position of Argentinian garrisons, dictated the advance across the fifty miles of country to Port Stanley. It must have been as evident to General Menendez as it was to military analysts beyond the Falklands that the British approach would be by a classic pincer movement, one hook of the pincers closing from the north and then east via Teal Inlet, Douglas Settlement and Mount Kent, the other from the south and then east via Goose Green and Darwin, Fitzroy and Bluff Cove. Meanwhile, a few units, mostly squadrons of the S.A.S., would move due east, across the higher, rougher and boggier ground in the middle of the island.

From S.A.S. and S.B.S. patrols and aerial reconnaissance Brigadier Thompson knew of every important enemy position; little more than an observation post of a few men could have remained hidden from the wide-ranging and thorough patrols.

The Argentinian commander at Goose Green, Air Commodore Wilson Drozier Pedrozo, and his senior military officer, Lieutenant-Colonel Halo Piaggi, knew that the British would be coming, if only because the route to Port Stanley via Goose Green was easier than the northern one. Their positions were strongly sited, with troops in defensive positions six kilometres deep. At the base, south of Goose Green airstrip, were anti-aircraft guns, which could be used as conventional artillery with devastating effect. The heavy mortars were well concealed and on the airstrip were some Pucara ground-attack aircraft. Machine-gunners were well dug in across the narrow isthmus along which any attack must come, for there was water on both sides. At the north end of the isthmus, a mile from Goose Green, was Darwin, from where the Argentinians planned to hit the advancing British with flanking fire. Apart from all these advantages, the British would have to advance across mostly open ground. In the settlement itself the Argentinians had locked into the civic hall 114 men, women and children of the settlement. They had been in captivity for a month and there was no way they could help the British when they came. Most importantly Pedrozo had 1,400 men by the time of the assault; the British were reckoning on only about 600. But Goose Green had been recently reinforced from Port Stanley. With British ships firing 4.5 inch shells into the Goose Green positions and Harriers dropping cluster bombs Pedrozo knew that he was being softened up for an attack.

Thompson and his staff decided to send marines and 3rd Parachute Battalion along the northern route towards Port Stanley while the capture of Darwin and Goose Green was entrusted to 2 Para, led by Lieutenant-Colonel Herbert Jones, affectionately known in the army as 'H'. Jones, aged forty-two, was a commanding officer in the dashing, heroic mould. He was tough himself and did not buy popularity but

103

was nevertheless enormously popular; the troops knew him as an officer who could always keep his cool in a tight corner and who lived by the regiment's motto, *Utrinque Paratus* – 'Ready for anything'.

Faced with the inevitability of a frontal attack Colonel Jones did his best to minimise the risk by making a pincer movement – restricted by the narrow isthmus – while sending a company across Choiseul Sound to attack the Argentinian positions from the rear.

'Advance to contact' was the order and the action began on the night of 26–27 May when an advance company of paras crossed the 900 foot Sussex Mountains and moved forward eight miles to two wooden-walled buildings known as Camilla House, overlooking Brenton Loch. The company's job was to secure the jumping off point for the battalion attack. Three other companies of 120 men moved up during the 27th, reaching their positions in darkness. Sea King helicopters lifted in two 105mm guns and the unit's 81mm mortars. The attack was launched, under cover of a naval bombardment, on Friday 28th at 2 a.m. As the Paras moved across the open ground, using stones as cover, and firing their Sterling sub-machine-guns and self-loading rifles, they came under heavy artillery fire, small arms fire and 30mm anti-aircraft cannon. This pressure was relieved when three R.A.F. GR3 Harriers came in fast and low and dropped cluster bombs on the gun emplacement. Even so, heavy mortar shells forced the paras to ground many times.

The paras crossed Camilla Creek and by 6 a.m. had taken Coronation Point and Darwin. Some Argentinians retreated towards Goose Green. The first enemy line of resistance was from Boca House to the Hill of Gorse and it resisted strongly before the paras broke through.

Argentinian Pucara planes and Skyhawk bombers strafed the Paras but lost four planes to the shoulder-fired Blowpipe missiles. A Pucara brought down a Marine scout helicopter, killing the pilot, Lieutenant Richard Nunn, who had been spotting for the paras. Without him the paras were deprived of their 'seeing eye'.

An Argentinian post raised a white flag and a para officer went forward with an escort to take the expected surrender. Instead, Argentinian machine-gunners opened up on this party and the officer was killed. This type of attack has angered soldiers down the centuries and the paras were no different; They shot down the troops involved in the incident and distrusted white flags from then on.

Near the Hill of Gorse a machine-gun post which the paras could not knock out held up their attack for half an hour. It was the type of critical moment, known to all fighting soldiers, when an attack can falter and perhaps fail. Normally, a C.O. remains a little further back, with his headquarters staff, to direct an action; it is not usually considered his duty to attack machine-gun posts in person. But Colonel Jones believed in leading from the front; with a Sterling sub-machine-gun in his hands, he ordered seven men to follow him in a headlong attack on the machine-gun nest. They ran and zigzagged and rolled to make themselves difficult targets and all the time they kept on firing. Unit mortars were giving covering fire and Jones and his men were about to reach their objective when he fell, as did his adjutant, Captain David Wood. The survivors completed the job, the gun was silenced and the attack went forward under Major Chris Keeble, who assumed command.

Again held up, the paras called for air strikes and three Harriers dropped cluster bombs on the Argentinians. One of the pilots was Squadron Leader Bob Iveson whose Harrier was shot down on his second sortie of the day, while raking Argentinian positions with cannonfire. Ejecting, Iveson came down a few miles from Goose Green and sheltered in an empty farmhouse. He was picked up by a patrolling helicopter two days later.

Major Keeble made radio contact with the Argentinian commander at 4 p.m. and a cease-fire was arranged. As night was falling the cease-fire could not be ensured and the paras spent a tense night. The cease-fire did not hold and sporadic firing continued throughout the night.

The surrender meeting was organised by two Falklanders, Alan Miller, manager of the Port San Carlos settlement and Eric Goff, manager at Goose Green. With their short wave transmitters they made it possible for the enemy commanders to talk. The surrender ceremony took place at 2.50 p.m., under the watchful eyes of paras posted to ensure that there was no last-minute change of mind. Major Keeble permitted Air Commodore Pedrozo to make an emotional political speech to his large force of men. They sang their national anthem – 'O hear, ye mortals, the sacred call . . .' – after which they threw down their arms and helmets, many with cheers of relief. For the first time the paras realised just how many prisoners they had taken, in addition to large quantities of rifles and machine-guns, two Pucaras, three 105mm howitzers and four 30mm anti-aircraft guns. And for the first time the Argentinians realised just how few British had captured them. A few officers told Spanish-speaking islanders that they had been 'shamed'. It was an unconscious tribute to Colonel Jones who had planned the entire operation, only to die in his superb act of valour and leadership, worthy of the Victoria Cross.

Robert Fox of the B.B.C. described how the paras brought the body of their C.O. down from the bloody place where he had fallen, with an N.C.O. marching in front with his rifle reversed, muzzle towards the ground, the military recognition of honourable death.

A soldier who witnessed this moving little ritual said, 'It was the saddest thing I ever saw, and I bet the paras were sad, but they didn't show it. I suppose they knew "H" wouldn't want them to.'

'H' Jones and his dead paras were taken back to San Carlos and with Flight-Lieutenant Nunn and a sapper of 59 Field Squadron, Royal Engineers, they were buried in a common grave. The chaplain of 2 Para, Padre David Cooper, read out the names of the dead as at a roll call. Robert Fox who witnessed the ceremony, said, 'At the end, the R.S.M. threw a handful of earth into the grave and marines and paras saluted in silence.' It was fitting that Fox was present; he had been as much in the front line at Goose Green as any para and his despatches were graphic and eloquent.

In London, Colonel Christopher Dumphie, Chief of Staff to the Military Deputy to the Commander-in-Chief Fleet, said of the Goose Green battle that 'it is probably one of the most brilliant and courageous actions conducted by a battalion since World War II'. It was certainly on a level with already famous battalion actions in Korea, Cyprus, Aden, Malaya and Northern Ireland.

The battle of Goose Green led to three controversies, all of which would linger for a long time. In the first place the paras had suffered seventeen dead and thirty-one wounded while the Argentinians lost 250 dead and 121 wounded. Normally in an infantry battle the wounded will exceed the dead by about three to one, perhaps two to one, though I have known equal proportions, and one case where every soldier on one side was killed. The Argentine force at Goose Green had lost twice as many dead as wounded. The discrepancy did not escape the notice of former frontline soldiers and of 'experts' who had not seen battle. Some of these experts, notably Americans, were quick to condemn the paras for 'bloodlust', though there was little evidence of this. War correspondents insisted that the paras took no reprisals for either the treachery of the white flag incident or in anger at the death of their beloved battalion commander, though neither would surprise veterans.

The assumption of bloodlust arose from another equally quick assumption. A company of marines had been hastily assembled and flown to Goose Green from San Carlos. There was speculation that the marines had been taken in to restrain the paras. This was not so. The fact is that the paras, finding greater opposition than expected, had no reserves to leave at dangerous spots as they pressed on with their attack; the marines were rushed in to hold Camilla Creek and to protect the paras' rear. Apart from this, had the paras already been involved in 'bloodlust' killing, all would have been over long before the marines arrived.

The large number of Argentinian dead can be accounted for on logical grounds. First, the experienced paras had fought a hard, uncompromising battle. Colonel Jones and others had trained them to be efficient and tough and it was this professional hardness which brought about their selection for Falklands service in the first place. More accurate with small arms fire than many other infantry units, it is not surprising that the paras inflicted more casualties than they received and that they fired killing rather than wounding shots. Apart from this, medical evidence I have received suggests that many of the dead Argentinians picked up at Goose Green had been killed by the cluster bombs which had been showering them for days. The wounds of many, I am told, were caused by shell splinters rather than by bullets.

Finally, some Argentinians who might have survived undoubtedly died because of their treachery with the white flag. After such an incident opposing soldiers shoot first; this is well known to fighting men. In the heat of action they cannot afford the luxury of the moralising judgments made by people 8,000 miles from the war.

As was to be expected the Argentinian propagandists exploited their high casualties. One newspaper screamed its abuse with BRITISH ASSASSINS' MASSACRE OF PRISONERS. Another: BRITISH MURDER SURVIVORS AS THEY SURRENDER.

The second controversy occurred over the view, held by Col. Jones, among others, that the B.B.C. World Service and the Ministry of Defence had announced that the paras were going to Goose Green. Colonel Jones assumed that the Argentinians had strengthened the Goose Green positions because of the B.B.C. report and told reporters with him on the attack that after the war he intended to sue the B.B.C. for manslaughter. It is a fact that the defences were stronger after the B.B.C. report than before it. There was widespread bitter feeling at San Carlos and Goose Green that not only the B.B.C. but politicians and newspapers were showing a reckless disregard for security.

A third controversy arose when more then thirty large aerial napalm bombs were found on and near Goose Green airstrip. There was, officers said, a napalm 'factory' including drums of napalm gel, mixing instructions and scores of drop tanks made into bombs. Napalm works in two ways – by bursting into ferocious flames which engulf men and machines and by sucking the oxygen from trenches and buildings so that those who escape the flames are suffocated. Napalm sticks to the skin, thus aggravating the burns.

The British should not too quickly condemn the Argentinians for barbarity; British troops on South Georgia had planned to use fire bombs against the

Argentinians, in an emergency, and British Harriers did use the no less horrific cluster bombs. Neither Britain nor Argentina had ratified a UN convention to outlaw incendiary weapons. Napalm became an emotive issue after its use in Vietnam but flame throwers were used in both the World Wars and the author of this book, in common with many other soldiers, used Molotov cocktails which were thrown at tanks in which the crews were burnt to death if they did not get out in time. Japanese positions in the Pacific were often destroyed by flame throwers.

The battle for Goose Green proved, as had the S.A.S. raid on Pebble Island, that technology in the shape of computers, lasers and lock-on missiles, already so much used in the Falklands war, could not replace the skill and courage of the infantryman. Reduced to its one essential – the need to take ground – victory could only be achieved by men prepared to go in on foot and fight.

As the fourteen-hour battle ended at Goose Green Surgeon-Commander Rick Jolly quickly set up a surgery and hospital in a disused refrigeration plant at Ajax Bay. His services were needed for Goose Green was a dangerous place with large quantities of unstable explosive, the napalm bombs and large amounts of assorted ammunition. Explosions did occur, wounding Argentinian and British soldiers. It was at first thought that Argentine booby traps had blown up but later it seemed that Argentine bombs had gone off while being moved. Other wounded were taken to British hospital ships.

Unwounded prisoners protested about not being quickly moved from Goose Green. They feared counter-attacks from their own air force and they had been suffering from cold and winter ailments for so long that they wanted to get to the greater comfort of British prisoner of war camps and ships. Many were taken to the landing ship *Sir Percival* and other British merchant vessels and herded into the ships' holds, converted into barracks. Here they crouched in rows while they were stripped, searched and documented. To satisfy the 1949 Geneva Convention's instruction that POWs must be identified the British scoured the civilian ship until they found labels used by the P and O civilian staff for passengers' luggage.

The 114 islanders who had been locked up without adequate food, water and sanitation, returned to their homes to find many of them vandalised; in some Argentinians had smeared excrement over the floor and had looted much personal property. Those Falklanders under lock and key may have been safer than those not held captive; some found themselves trapped in the Goose Green fire fight. Shells landed close to their homes and bullets had riddled their walls.

While the 2nd Parachute Battalion had been making for Port Stanley via Goose Green, the 3rd Battalion, with marine commandos, moved out of San Carlos on 27 May towards Douglas and Teal Inlet. They were captured in a much less dramatic fashion than Goose Green but with even more display of the British footsoldier's professionalism. Some of the marines and paras flew in by helicopter but most made the trip by 'yomping', the marines' slang for their form of forced marching while carrying as much as 120 lb of combat gear. The marines marched by night for six hours or more at a time through sleet, snow and heavy rain. Occasionally they found refuge in farm buildings but more often they slept outdoors and ate cold food to avoid betraying their positions with fires. The forty-mile march took the Argentinians by surprise; unable themselves to move around the boggy islands even by vehicles, they were astonished – as prisoners admitted – to find that the British had marched through such difficult country.

The British also showed their superiority in night fighting, a form of combat which the Argentinians feared. Under direct military pressure and the psychological pressure of fear, they fell back towards Stanley. Helicopters brought in loads of men and heavy weapons, flying as close to the ground as possible. To the surprise of the British command General Menendez and his staff had failed to hold Mount Kent, the commanding height of 1,504 feet only ten miles from the capital. Working in snow, British gunners overnight installed mortars and 105mm guns on the mountain and were in a position to shell almost any position between themselves and the town.

Before any final decision to launch a devastating attack, which would inevitably mean many deaths, Admiral Woodward tried one last ploy to induce General Menendez to surrender. Over the Argentinian positions Harriers dropped leaflets, with a safe-conduct pass on one side and an open letter to the Argentinian commander on the other. Written in Spanish and signed by Woodward, it read: 'We are both aware of the serious military situation which now confronts you and your men. There can be no prospect of your garrison being relieved. Matters have now reached the point where you must consider whether there is any further point in maintaining resistance in the face of such overwhelming odds.'

Menendez did not reply. It was not to be expected that he would but Admiral Woodward was right to make the appeal to common sense, if only to anticipate the widespread protest that would follow when the Argentinians in Port Stanley were bombarded. Menendez needed heavy casualties among his own troops, just as the Junta leaders needed casualties. How could they prove to their own people that they had been brave leaders unless they sacrificed young men on the altar of their own vanity.

9 Through Fire and Water to Stanley

Within his Puerto Argentino (Port Stanley) perimeter General Menendez had all the advantages of the defender over the attacker. He had no lines of communication to worry about protecting; all his ammunition and stores were close at hand. His men had been in position for two months and there had been plenty of time for them to dig themselves into winter-proof trenches and dugouts. His artillery of 105mm, 155mm guns and the infantry mortars had been ranged, so that the gunners knew the exact distance to likely targets on sea and land. The general's HQ staff had planned successive lines of defence so that should one be breached the troops could fall back to the next. And the best troops – the marine commandos – were in position where the fighting might be the hardest.

Transport was not a major problem for within the relatively small area held by the Argentinians most movement could be by foot; but if necessary trucks were available, together with the Swiss Mowag Roland, a small four-wheeled vehicle designed for rough country in which three or four infantrymen could take up position with a 7.62mm machine-gun. In addition, the Argentinians had the LARC, the modern version of the World War II amphibious DUKW. For as long as the men of the

Stanley garrison remained in prepared positions, they had the advantage over any attacking force that must approach over ground which in daylight gave practically no cover.

The Argentinians had another inestimable advantage – their long-range Westinghouse radar equipment on Two Sisters Ridge and Sapper Hill. Mobile and sophisticated, the Westinghouse system has a range of more than 250 miles. The British tried repeatedly to knock out the two posts, which could give warning of British ship movements.

In contrast with Menendez, General Moore had many disadvantages. His troops had to reach the hills west of Stanley across extremely difficult ground and they had to take everything with them, enough for what might prove to be a long campaign. With winter becoming more severe by the day the soldiers' health and fitness could become a major problem. The supporting fleet was still terribly vulnerable to air attack, as were the British helicopters. The only secure British base was San Carlos, fifty miles from Stanley, with a secondary base at Goose Green, vulnerable to air attack. Moore had 3,000 fresh troops – Brigadier Wilson's 5th Brigade – but at the end of May how they would reach Stanley had not been decided.

The Argentine air force was a greater danger to the British than the British planes of the navy and R.A.F. were to the Argentinians; there were no Argentine ships for the British planes to attack. While Menendez could manipulate his manpower, easily moving reserves to any threatened part of the front, Moore needed every fit man moving forward. The

116

British had so many prisoners that a volunteer platoon of 'Blue Berets' – including cooks, mechanics and stewards – was landed to help guard them at San Carlos. Under a supply officer, the Blue Berets came from H.M.S. *Hermes* and their presence enabled the British H.Q. staff to relieve valuable fighting men from guard duty.

Moore had yet another acute worry – the safety of the Falkland islanders remaining in Port Stanley. Intelligence reports indicated that most would probably shelter in the few stone buildings during the shelling but it was always possible that shells which undershot or overshot their targets would land in the town.

Woodward and Moore faced a task which their professional peers might envy and fear at the same time. Capturing Port Stanley was a mission which any senior career officer would welcome as an opportunity to demonstrate his skill. But general and admiral had to prise thousands of enemy soldiers away from a wooden, highly inflammable town occupied by civilians. Apart from this local difficulty, they were performing in the world's spotlight before a formidable front-row audience of experienced critics, political and military, who would tear their reputations to shreds if they failed, or even if they lost too many lives in succeeding.

But they did have one priceless advantage over Menendez – the brilliant victory at Goose Green. In British ears the name Goose Green – before the battle took place there – had an unreal sound, like some ancient village in rural England where the most exciting event of the year was the annual fair; even after the battle the name would not look quite fitting on a roll of battle honours. But to General Menendez and his men, thirty-five miles to the east, it must have had an ominous sound when they heard – as they did – about the 'Red Devils' who had taken the settlement against overwhelming odds. We know that officers told the ordinary soldiers just the opposite – that the British had been the overwhelming force in numbers.

In Britain by 2 June there began to appear in letters to editors a curious desire to allow the Argentinians to surrender with honour. As a tactical measure – to save British casualties – this had something to commend it but the letter writers seemed to be proposing the idea on the grounds of outmoded chivalry. Lord Young of Dartington wrote to *The Times* on 2 June hoping that '... before the final assault on Port Stanley there is a pause, and that the Argentine forces are given the opportunity of an honourable withdrawal ... It is what all the great generals in history would have done.'

They would have done nothing of the kind. With victory within their grasp the great generals of history, up to and including those of the Korean War, wanted that victory to be complete. In earlier times a victorious general might have permitted a defeated army to leave the field with its colours flying but that was only after it really had been defeated – and sometimes it was done to emphasise the defeat. 'Honourable withdrawals' do not exist except as a feeble fiction to disguise a defeat and then the notion is suggested by the vanquished rather than the victor.

On the same day as Lord Young's letter Mrs

Thatcher ruled out any magnanimity but she did say that if the Argentinians decided within the following few days to withdraw they would be given ten to fourteen days to do so.

And all the time the weather was getting worse, imposing greater strains on the soldiers. Prime Minister and Commander had great confidence in the men's ability to withstand winter's rigors and it was a major factor in decision making. The confidence was well founded.

The climate of the Falklands has been described as resembling that of the Outer Hebrides in winter. The danger to soldiers came from the drenching rain, the relentless wind and the unpredictability of the weather. The dry cold of Norway, said the soldiers who had trained there, was infinitely preferable to the wet cold of the Falklands. The 3rd Battalion Parachute Regiment made a thirty-six-hour march across rough country to Teal Inlet, fording two rivers, splashing through dozens of streams and slogging through marshes. Travelling light, they left sleeping bags, waterproofs and rucksacks to be helicoptered in. Their only nourishment was the iron rations carried in their pockets. Several suffered from exposure and foot injuries.

The marines used the 'buddy' system as part of their survival technique. In the icy mountains all men were paired off and each was responsible for keeping a constant watch on his partner for symptoms such as drowsiness, lassitude, unusual pallor and 'strange' behaviour, all of which could indicate frostbite or imminent collapse from exposure. The sufferer would at once get 'the treatment' – such as massage of arms and legs. Cases of exposure were more frequent than reported and when a soldier was known to be suffering he was placed in a transparent plastic bag – the 'survival bag' – in just his long underwear. His body heat, unable to escape through the plastic, helped him to recover.

Some of the men advancing towards Stanley were, soldier-fashion, making macabre jests, sometimes about the 1,000 rubber coffins carried in the *Atlantic Conveyor* and now at the bottom of the sea. 'I'd have liked the idea of being buried in rubber,' one para said. 'Means I'll bounce back.'

The dogged courage of the marines and paras and of the engineers and gunners who joined them on the hills on the Port Stanley perimeter was impressive and well recorded by the correspondents with them. The real heroes of the pre-battle period, the helicopter pilots, received less attention. They did not have to grind their way through peat bog but they did spend ten unbroken hours each day and every day in their seats, whether flying from the navy's assault ships or from land bases. The choppers' thrashing rotor blades were the constant background noise of the Falklands war.

Helicopters were the most indispensable weapon. In the swamp and roadless wastes of the Falklands dynamic military action would have been impossible without them. In every possible hour of flying time a great weight of equipment was brought up from San Carlos, slung in nets from the bellies of Sea King and Wessex helicopters – thousands of mortar rounds, thousands of boxes of ammunition for machine guns and rifles, tents, vast quantities of field rations, spare weapons, bridging equipment and road strengthening material. Getting a 105mm gun to the top of Mount Kent, for instance, could have taken days of exhausting work involving many men and using up trucks. A helicopter lifted an artillery piece weighing 5,000 lb to the mountain in an hour or so. Only rarely did a helicopter fail to take off because of the weather, appalling though it often was. Pilots and crews drove themselves to exhaustion to meet the pressing needs of army and navy; several times a medical officer or a squadron commander would be forced to order a particular crew to spend a day in bed. At night mechanics serviced the helicopters, sometimes by torchlight, so that throughout the war most of the aircraft were airworthy most of the time. The main fear of the helicopter pilot, particularly early in the campaign, was that of being spotted and attacked by a Pucara, but being slow and virtually unarmed, the helicopters could also be brought down by small-arms fire.

On Saturday 6 June General Moore sent a despatch to London: 'I don't want us dashing in there [Port Stanley] causing unnecessary loss of life to my soldiers, which nobody back in Britain or here would like to see. We will do it in a proper, sensible, well-balanced military way.'

General Moore's 'military way' was to steadily squeeze the Argentinian defences, first with bold raids, then with battalion attacks on various arcs of the enemy front. Meanwhile naval and air bombardment would depress the morale of the defenders. From early in the campaign a basic and consistent tactic was to deprive the Argentinians of sound sleep with naval bombardment by night. Going without sleep for long periods, under the harassing noise of bursting shells, is quickly demoralising even for hardened troops. Finally General Moore would move his whole line forward in one or possibly two major attacks, by night and by surprise. In this progressive way, combining demoralisation with infantry assault, he hoped to avoid the costly losses in life which generally result from a precipitate all-out frontal assault. From the reports of his patrols the general knew the points at which he could most profitably strike; one idea was to hit the lines of Los Primeros, an élite Argentinian unit. If these men could be broken the blow to the conscript units would be devastating.

But Moore's timing had to be nicely judged; he could not keep his troops in their cold, wet trenches until they became too tired and unfit to perform as first-rate fighting men. To reinforce 2 and 3 Para and the marines he started to land Brigadier Tony Wilson's 5th Brigade (Scots Guards, Welsh Guards and Gurkhas) at San Carlos on 1 June. How the brigade would reach the battlefront had not then been decided but since the British northern pincer was strong enough it was thought that the Guards and the Gurkhas would be moved around the south to support the battle-depleted 2 Para.

On the icy heights conditions in the freezing wet trenches were as bad as those faced by the British troops in the Crimea in the winter of 1854–5 and on Gallipoli in November 1915. Bitter winds drove slanting rain into everything and 'waterproof' clothing only delayed the water from reaching the skin; it couldn't stop it. The commandos strengthened their slit trenches against the weather and the enemy with rocks, old boxes and plastic but comfort was impossible. Fortunately, there was sometimes a large sheep-shearing shed where troops could snatch some sleep while on rotation out of the trenches.

Some Falkland families, finding themselves in the middle of a battle area, refused to be evacuated and turned their homes into combat catering centres, providing tea and toasted sandwiches – and a warm-up in front of the fire – for all-comers. Some provided a visitors' book; a repatriated soldier told me that he had seen such comments as 'Ta very much', 'This is a corner of an English field', and '*Après la guerre* I'll come back'.

The S.A.S. and S.B.S. made more of their shadowy raids, usually after a radio message from one of their scouts, living rough in the hills for days on end. The scout would report that a group of Argentinians had dug in at some vantage point. Whether it was a job for the S.A.S. or S.B.S. sometimes depended on whether a 'rigid raider' assault craft was needed. The rigid raiders are plastic flat-bottom craft that skim the water at forty mph. If so, the S.B.S. would mount the pre-dawn attack on the unsuspecting enemy. Provided the Argentinians surrendered very quickly they became prisoners and were taken off to the nearest pen. Virtually every objective was examined – 'recced' as soldiers put it – by the S.A.S. and S.B.S. before a major attack began. The S.A.S. frequently complained that whenever Argentinian troops spotted them they 'legged it'.

In this war, as in others, raiding and patrolling was a kind of tense and deadly adventure. A reconnaissance patrol from the Scots Guards ran into an Argentine patrol and killed nine of them before breaking off contact; the only British casualty was the young officer in command, who was shot in the hand. The stealthy Gurkhas were used to clear enemy observation posts from the hilltops overlooking the track between Darwin and Stanley, thus depriving the Argentinians of information about the British build-up. Gurkhas, paras, commandos ... after each patrol the men needed twelve hours drying out in regimental aid post tents.

By 2 June the British troops had advanced to within seven miles of Port Stanley, thus bringing the garrison under increasingly heavy artillery bombardment. The gun teams of 29 Commando Regiment Royal Artillery were even shelling the Argentine positions in the Moody Brook barracks, the former base of the marine base in Port Stanley. In the first week of June the Argentinians managed only two desultory raids against the task force; in one a Skyhawk was believed to have been shot down. In the other an Argentine C-130 Hercules transport tried to bomb a British tanker. Airmen on the makeshift bomber simply pushed the bombs out a cargo door. One bomb bounced off the tanker, causing no damage. Argentine arms buyers were frantically scouring the world for new weapons, especially Exocets and the planes to carry them. But no weapons could solve the problems of the Argentinians on the ground in Port Stanley; the return fire on

British positions on Mount Kent was ineffective.

Then General Menendez brought his troops so far in from their original perimeter that the move took the British by surprise. But it was a welcome surprise, even if it had disrupted the first plans for attack. British staff officers could see no reason why Menendez made this withdrawal from key positions unless it was in expectation that he would be forced back anyway. In pulling back Menendez shortened his line, tightening it into a classic horse-shoe shape, normally a particularly tough form of defence to break.

In fact, Menendez was beginning to lose confidence in his troops. And he had reason to. Morale was falling, many of the younger soldiers were homesick, not much mail was getting through – though a couple of radio channels were open for soldiers to speak to their families – and some officers were proving poor leaders. Not enough provision had been made for medical care of the troops, a sign of the Argentinian High Command's belief that the British fleet would be driven off and that no serious land fighting would take place. At least Menendez had the satisfaction of knowing that the British blockade was being broken; aircraft were making the run from Argentina and on at least one occasion a ship got through. The British, through some lapse in field intelligence, knew little of this. One minor mystery of the campaign is why the British never did gain possession of the Argentine Order of Battle, even with 2,000 prisoners in their hands to interrogate and with the ability to get special service troops into Port

Stanley clandestinely. Perhaps the lack of experienced Spanish-speaking intelligence officers was the main difficulty.

Perhaps it was just as well that General Moore did not know the full strength of the Stanley garrison. By every military rule he was taking a big chance in attacking with only about 6,000; military practice demands that an attacking force be at least twice as strong as the defenders. And Goose Green had been a sharp lesson. Despite their defeat, the conscripts at Goose Green had shown themselves willing and able to resist fiercely from fortified positions. In this, the Argentinians, so many of whom were of Italian stock, were fighting in the Italian way, so reminiscent of World War II. The Italians often fought fiercely for short periods but would then break suddenly and surrender at the first sign of bloody defeat.

On 7 June, for the first time, the Queen referred in public to the Falklands conflict, as she opened the Kielder Dam in Northumberland. Her voice filled with unusual emotion, she said, 'Our thoughts today are with those who are in the South Atlantic and our prayers are for their success and a safe return to their homes and loved ones.'

The very next day another tragedy struck the task force the worst blow of the campaign. As has been explained, the 5th Brigade had already landed but a second bridgehead was needed to bring these troops into an attack from the south, in the process bypassing the dominant height of Two Sisters Ridge.

Brigadier Wilson, making a reconnaissance beyond Darwin, was lucky enough to establish radio contact with a farmer at Fitzroy, along the coast towards Port Stanley. He learnt that no Argentinian troops were at Fitzroy or Bluff Cove. As it happened, several residents of Fitzroy had travelled to Port Stanley to get essential supplies and were allowed through. The military presence there was obvious enough, with armoured cars, jeeps, machine-gun posts and stacks of ammunition, but enemy troops had pulled back from Fitzroy. The brigadier seized the opportunity. Commandeering a Chinook and smaller helicopters he crowded them with about a hundred troops and rushed them to Bluff Cove where they quickly dug in, just defeating nightfall.

Next morning, Sunday 6 June, he had his first reinforcements, Scots Guardsmen landed from the H.M.S *Intrepid*. As the open landing craft ferried them ashore Argentinian gunners fired star shells above them and the already tense men, exposed under the flares, feared imminent air attack. No attack eventuated but the incident was a warning that the Argentinians knew of the Guards' arrival. The *Intrepid*'s approach may have been observed on the big Westinghouse radar on the hills behind Bluff Cove.

Still with the advantage of low cloud and mist, Brigadier Wilson moved more of his Welsh Guards and Scots Guards forward from San Carlos to Lively Island; from here the landing ships *Sir Galahad* and *Sir Tristram* would bring them into the narrow inlet of Port Pleasant where they would disembark on the shallow landing craft.

The landing ships, each crewed by nineteen British officers and fifty Hong Kong ratings, were important and versatile craft. Each of 5,670 tons, they could carry up to 540 troops with their heavy equipment, including twenty Wessex helicopters or sixteen main battle tanks or more than thirty other vehicles, as well as thirty tons of ammunition and much fuel.

That night, 6 June, a long and interesting voice report by Michael Nicholson reached London and was passed by the MoD; it was published in London on Monday morning, 7 June. The most significant paragraph read: 'There are underway at this moment operations which I can only describe as extraordinarily daring which cannot be revealed until they are completed, but which, if they are successful will certainly bring the end of this war that much closer. Hopefully, we shall be able to report them soon.'

The pregnant tone of this paragraph would have excited even the dullest of enemy intelligence agents and base intelligence analysts. They would at once ask themselves *where* such vital operations could be taking place and *what type* of operations they could be. Since an airborne attack was virtually impossible in such weather in this terrain it had to be a seaborne landing. The number of landing places was limited and Bluff Cove was one of the more obvious.

The Russians, through their hovering satellite might well have picked up the voice report and relayed it to the Argentinians, or perhaps the approaching *Sir Galahad* and *Sir Tristram* were spotted on the big radar. Just why the landing of a large part of 5th Brigade was made without the usual air cover may not emerge for some time; a possibility is that Admiral Woodward could not risk warships in the extremely confined waters off Bluff Cove. Another is that Brigadier Wilson took a calculated risk, believing that he could get his men ashore before the enemy could react and before the weather cleared.

Violent storms made the ships late to Fitzroy on Tuesday 8 June – but they also lifted the clouds. *Sir Galahad* and *Sir Tristram* anchored under an open sky, in broad daylight, with many men aboard. The British air defences, Rapier batteries and Blowpipes of No 63 Squadron, Royal Air Force Regiment, were unloaded by helicopter during the morning and their crews were hurriedly setting them up on the hillside overlooking the water. At 2 p.m. they still needed another hour to be ready for action. *Sir Tristram* had unloaded most of her troops but *Sir Galahad* was still crowded with busy but relaxed soldiers.

At 2 p.m. four Argentinian planes – two Mirages and two Skyhawks – flying at little more than masthead height flashed in 'out of nowhere'. They were first seen by soldiers on the beach who frantically fired their rifles and sub-machine-guns as a way of sounding the alarm. They had reacted quickly but it was too late.

Sir Tristram was hit by rockets and cannon-fire and heavy bombs hit *Sir Galahad* aft and through the accommodation section. Flames quickly erupted, setting off ammunition. Men rushed to the ship's side and scrambled down ropes into rubber liferafts. Some of these were blown by the wind into patches of burning oil while others, hit by hot debris, burst into flames. When the ship's fuel tanks exploded the *Sir Galahad* was enveloped in thick black smoke, trapping many men still aboard the ship. In this dire emergency Sea King and Wessex helicopter pilots went straight into the smoke while their crewmen winched down on lines to pluck men from the deck or from the sea. On a day of heroism the helicopter pilots stood out as particularly and repeatedly courageous.

Correspondents and soldiers, watching helplessly from the beach and cliffs, saw helicopters carry out what must surely be one of the most ingenious helicopter rescues on record. Four pilots had noticed that some orange liferafts carrying survivors, including wounded, were being sucked towards the stern of the *Sir Galahad* by the roaring flames on the ship and on the water, which were creating a furious updraught; the air-filled craft were in danger of being engulfed by fire. The pilots positioned their helicopters to the rear of the blazing ship, in thick smoke and dangerously close to the flames. Tilting forward they used their giant blades and slowly blew the liferafts away from the flames to safety. This was cool-headed bravery at its best.

To the soldiers already ashore, watching in shocked and mesmerised horror, Port Pleasant was a fearful sight, with lifeboats, orange inflatable rafts and landing craft ferrying ashore survivors and injured, some of whom were screaming in agony. Soldiers ran into the freezing water to take their shocked and wounded mates onto their shoulders. At the top of the beach armoured car crews strapped them to their vehicles and drove them to the field hospital. From here they were helicoptered back to the medical centre at San Carlos and within a few hours many were aboard the hospital ship *Uganda*.

A second enemy attack of five Skyhawks came in

130

about sundown to attack the men ashore with cluster bombs. This time there were no British casualties and some of the aircraft were hit and destroyed, probably by the Scots Guards.

On the same day a landing craft from H.M.S. *Fearless* was hit in Choiseul Sound and six men were killed, and the frigate H.M.S. *Plymouth* was hit by bombs, probably from a Skyhawk, and badly damaged, though no crew members were killed. The *Plymouth* put up a remarkable fight against a concentrated attack by four Mirage jets on the north side of East Falkland. During these raids seven Argentine planes were shot down and four others were possibly hit.

On this worst day of the war for Britain casualties were severe; fifty-six servicemen, mostly Welsh Guards, were killed and about a hundred were wounded, while others had minor injuries. On *Sir Galahad* three officers and two members of the crew were killed and two officers and nine crew members injured. On *Sir Tristram* two crew members were killed.

For the Argentinians the attack on Bluff Cove was a significant victory, since it put out of action two of the five British landing support ships and blasted the striking power of a major infantry unit. Two companies of marine commandos were brought forward to make good the loss of Welsh Guards in the Bluff Cove tragedy.

When the casualty figures for the Bluff Cove were slow in being released another row blew up between the MoD and the Press and between MoD and Downing Street. It was the old problem of how much to reveal and when, with all the accompanying ramifications. There was by now a recognised priority of disclosure but this had not been observed, so that Mrs Thatcher and her Defence Secretary had given different reasons why the casualty figures had not been announced.

The military men had a sound reason for withholding casualty figures. The jubilant Argentinians had already announced that 400 British troops had been killed or wounded in the Bluff Cove attack and it made sense to allow them to go on believing this. They would probably draw the conclusion that the British field commander could not now launch a major assault on Port Stanley for several days. Unfortunately, profoundly afraid of security leaks, MoD officials apparently could not bring themselves to explain the situation to the Press. Once again, the media and MoD need for education became clear; the media and MoD must learn more about the way the other works.

The Argentinians had not delayed the British build up. On the night of the devastating air raid at Bluff Cove a large force of paras crept to within 200 yards of key Argentinian positions without being detected. They were prepared for a battle if fired on but the operation was designed to test the enemy's degree of vigilance. It was not impressive.

While the men of the 5th Brigade were getting into position commando patrols were probing the Argentinian defences, attacking and clearing observation posts and calling for artillery fire on stronger units. Sappers of the Royal Engineers had particular hazards to face; they were dealing with

Argentinian mines planted to slow down the British infantry.

Many deeds of heroism occurred during the siege of Port Stanley. One which was praised by the troops themselves was performed by Royal Marine Leading Medical Assistant Steve Hayward. During an artillery barrage he brought to safety a marine whose foot had been blown off by a mine and used his own body to shield the wounded man from flying shell splinters.

Before the final battle the battle-hardened British troops felt sorry for the Argentinian teenage conscripts who made up such a large part of the garrison, but as they said, 'a gun in the hands of a boy can kill you just the same'. Their attitude was a characteristic mixture of compassion and hard realism. Officers reckoned that after one look at the wild-looking, dirty and unshaven British troops, coming out of the hills like avenging furies, the younger Argentinians would run away. Charles Laurence of the *Daily Telegraph* thought they would scare even the Vikings.

General Moore's staff, principally his deputy, Brigadier John Waters, and his chief of staff, Colonel Ian Baxter, were completing their plans to breach the Argentinian defences. In Argentina at that moment Pope John Paul was talking to General Galtieri, Admiral Anaya and Brigadier Dozo. In his papal balancing-act, he was trying to show the Argentinians that he had not taken Britain's side – or any side – in the war. The Pope's visit gave Galtieri his best chance of withdrawing from the war with honour.. The dictator had only to say that he was obeying the Pope's plea to stop the fighting; had he done this he could have stayed in office with dignity and power undiminished. Apparently Galtieri was neither imaginative enough nor intelligent enough to seize this last chance.

That night, Friday 11 June, British ships bombarded pre-determined Argentinian targets, helicopter gunships attacked Argentinian positions and 29 Commando Regiment Royal Artillery shelled the enemy. During these bombardments H.M.S. *Glamorgan,* giving supporting fire from offshore, was hit by a land-fired Exocet and thirteen sailors were killed, with seventeen injured. Ashore three Falkland islanders, all women, were caught in the bombardment and died from their wounds.

The troops were in position by 1 a.m. Officers made a final check on Argentine trenches and foxholes with the help of image-intensifiers – which use available light from the moon and stars to 'turn night into day' – before the assault began. The major objectives were the twin peaks of Two Sisters; it was also the most difficult ground because the slopes were strewn with boulders and scree which made silent movement almost impossible, and which could easily have concealed snipers and machine-gun posts.

Julian Thompson led 3 Commando Brigade and 3rd Parachute Regiment – 1,700 men – in a three-pronged attack to capture the intermediate arc of high ground west of Port Stanley. After fierce fighting, by dawn on Saturday 12 June 3 Para had captured Mount Longdon, 45 Commando had control of Two Sisters and 42 Commando of Mount Harriet. Most Argentinians did not know of their danger until the British infantry appeared among them, bayonets levelled, and they were terrified. Paratroopers were involved in possibly the heaviest fighting of the campaign with regular Argentinian commandos. Those Argentinians not killed or taken prisoner fell back to another defence line.

In this hard-fought phase of the battle the British lost twenty-five, eighteen of them paras, five marines and two Royal Engineers; sixty-two men were wounded. Many Argentinians were killed and 1,800 prisoners were taken. When the action finished the British had advanced two miles. After this blow General Menendez must have realised that he was beaten but he seems to have been in a fantasy world at this time, victim of his own rhetoric about fighting to the last man and the last bullet. In Buenos Aires the news was regarded so seriously that a live television coverage of a mass being celebrated by the Pope was interrupted to announce the British attack.

As is normal, the Commando Brigade consolidated its positions that day but at night patrols from both brigades – the 5th Infantry Brigade having joined the commandos – disturbed the Argentinians with aggressive patrolling and routes were reconnoitred for the next attack, which began on the night of 13–14 June.

The 4th Field Artillery and 29th Commando Regiment, Royal Artillery, heavily bombarded the enemy positions. Then 2 Para, already battle hardened from Goose Green, passed through 3 Para and captured Wireless Ridge. The Scots Guards attacked positions on Tumbledown Mountain, the Gurkhas took Mount William, and the Welsh

Guards, Sapper Hill. The British had lost six more men killed and seventeen wounded. The turning point in the battle had occurred when the Scots Guards captured the strong machine-gun posts at Tumbledown Mountain, which blocked the way to Sapper Hill. In six hours of bloody night fighting the Guards outfought the best Argentinian troops and opened the way to Stanley. Had they not taken the mountain before daylight Port Stanley town itself could have become the battlefield.

By midday on Monday the Argentinians, having again suffered heavy casualties, were in full retreat and soon white flags began to flutter in many places as groups of men hoisted handkerchiefs, underwear, pieces of sheeting and even bandages. British H.Q. had been broadcasting to Menendez's H.Q. for at least a week, trying to appeal to the Argentinian sense of humanity, dignity and honour. Colonel Michael Rose of the S.A.S., who had been in charge of breaking the Iranian Embassy siege and an expert in psychological warfare, planned the British verbal approach and it was put across by Captain Rod Bell, of the Royal Marines, a Spanish speaker. Bell and Rose were aware of the part played by Dr Alison Bleaney – the 'heroine of Port Stanley' – in urging the Argentinians to speak over the radio with the British about the safety of the Port Stanley civilians. This led to surrender negotiations.

Brigadier Waters arranged for a meeting between the opposing generals and after two hours the cease-fire was signed. More than 10,600 new prisoners throughout the Falklands fell into British hands. General Moore, probably conscious of having done a crisp, professional job of work, sent a signal to the command centre at Northwood, one of the few to arrive in clear language and not in code.

Headquarters Land Forces Falkland Islands. In Port Stanley at 9 o'clock p.m. Falkland time tonight, 14 June, surrendered to me all the Argentine armed forces in East and West Falkland, together with their impediments.

Arrangements are in hand to assemble the men for return to Argentina, to gather in their arms and equipment, and to mark and make safe their munitions. The Falkland Islands are once more under the Government desired by their inhabitants. God save the Queen.

Signed, J. J. Moore.

Nearly three months earlier Mrs Thatcher had asked her commanders to conclude the war by mid-June; they finished it on the 14th. The triumphant Prime Minister, relieved that her policy had been vindicated and proud of her fighting men, appears to have made no capital out of this interesting fulfilment of her request, as the Union flag was hoisted again in East and West Falkland. And Port Stanley had not been damaged in the fighting.

By an inspired decision, Major Mike Norman of 42 Commando Royal Marines was brought down from the hills to supervise the Argentinian surrender. His previous meeting with the enemy had been on 2 April, also in Port Stanley, when sheer weight of numbers had forced him to surrender. As he had arrived only four days earlier the experience was particularly unpleasant. It was his task to arrange for the collection of Argentinian weapons. To help him he had members of the marine company who had been captured with him ten weeks before. One was heard to say to a comrade, 'It occurs to me that we're still outnumbered about two to one by the Argies.' His friend replied, 'That would be right, but this time all I have to do is whistle and I'll have a Harrier overhead and a warship in the bay.'

Recriminations and fault-finding, inquiries and reports, cover-ups and excuses would follow. The Falklands affair would reverberate for years. But with Port Stanley recaptured, the whole of the Falklands recovered and the war won – even if the Argentinians refused to admit that they had lost it – one thing was clear. The British armed forces had shown the British nation why they existed. Two generations of Britons who had not before known war now knew the risks to which servicemen were exposed when they found themselves at war, and they could be proud of the bravery their sailors, soldiers and airmen had displayed.

They had shown, said Mrs Thatcher on Liberation Night, 'skill, determination and efficiency'. Indeed they had – as many had shown before in Northern Ireland. In the South Atlantic 25,000 servicemen had been stretched to the limit physically and mentally and came out of the ordeal with a maturity which older ex-fighting men would recognise.

There is something else. British blood has been spilled in the Falklands; 255 British bodies lie in the Falkland soil or the Falkland waters. To permit Argentina to play any part in the administration of the Falkland Islands would be to write off these men's sacrifice as worthless. No greater offence to the battle dead and their families can be imagined.* And it would make the men and women of the task force bitter; they would regard as a betrayal any agreement which would give Argentina a place in the Falklands. But even as the war ended, politicians in the United States, in Europe and even in Britain were saying, in effect, to the Government, 'Sooner or later you will have to reach some agreement with the Argentinians ... a postal service perhaps, air transport ... some kind of concession ... some form of accommodation ...' Political expediency is a powerful force but so is British public opinion – the Falklands war demonstrated that – and it might not tolerate 'concessions' and 'accommodations'.

Mrs Thatcher said that she would make the Falklands into a fortress, if necessary. I believe that she meant it. If any of her successors should hand over the keys of that fortress to Argentina I hope that the voting public will condemn them, that posterity will damn them and that the ghosts of 255 dead British servicemen will haunt them.

*Another 600 British were wounded; many of them would be crippled for life.

10 The Propaganda War

From the beginning the British should have been able to fight a better propaganda war than the Argentinians if only because of long experience and the advantage of natural understatement. Extravagant propaganda, which the Argentinians practised, is rarely effective externally, though when aimed by an administration at its own people it can have dramatic results, especially when those people are naturally volatile and emotional.

The Argentinians had some general objectives – to show that Britain was the aggressor, and by association that Argentina was the victim, to vilify Margaret Thatcher, to whip up Argentinian patriotic fervour for the war, to bring Latin American countries to their support, and to punish the United States for its 'betrayal' of Argentina. Sometimes a particular story was designed to achieve more than one end. But Argentinian propagandists never did succeed in designing a two-strand approach – one internal, the other external; perhaps they did not try. They produced a story and fired it broadside, hoping to hit something. One of the most ambitious was that Admiral Sandy Woodward had committed suicide because of his despair when the *Sheffield* was hit; another claimed the wounding and capture of Prince Andrew and a third – repeated several times – was the sinking of the flagship *Hermes*. Telam, the government press agency, even had Prince Andrew saying to the Queen, 'Mummy, I'm frightened; please don't send me to the war!' Finally, Prince Andrew was lost when the *Hermes* was destroyed and the Queen was in mourning for her lost prince; Telam produced a photograph of her in a dark dress to prove it. Prince Andrew took part in operational flying throughout the campaign and was never protected.

One aim of the propaganda in Argentina was to prepare the public for war, not negotiations. After the sinking of the *Belgrano* the navy did not want to negotiate – it had lost too many men and wanted to regain its honour by keeping the war going and fighting the British. (But it never did.)

Slogans were commonplace, especially 'Viva Argentina' or just 'Ar-gen-ti-na' chanted as at a football match. Another was 'May Argentina lead Latin America to victory!' Professional claquers were on hand to lead crowds into chanting 'Death to the pirates!' 'Viva Latin America!' 'Send the English into the sea!' A persistent line was to remind the Argentinians that in 1806, 1807 and 1845 the British had attempted to invade Argentine mainland and had always been repulsed. (No invasion took place in 1845. In 1806 five hundred troops were landed in an unauthorised attack.)

Propaganda directed against Mrs Thatcher was especially vitriolic; posters and magazine covers depicted her as a pirate wearing a headcloth with skull and crossbones and a patch over one eye; at other times she was shown as a witch and a vulture or as a new Hitler. In whatever guise her features were

141

touched up to make her ugly, a standard propaganda treatment for enemy leaders. One poster showed President Reagan with Mrs Thatcher in his arms in the style of Clark Gable and Vivien Leigh in *Gone With the Wind*. This drawing was just too good; all copies rapidly disappeared as collector's items. An issue of *Tal Cual*, a popular weekly scandal magazine, showed Mrs Thatcher on its cover with the fangs of a female Dracula. In an accompanying 'biography' of the Prime Minister she was 'The Dame of Death'.

Newspaper editors were told to practise 'self-censorship so that press censorship and other restrictions are not necessary'. The government also issued a decree against publishing any news that could 'damage the morale of the population'. Osiris Troiani, a political commentator on Radio Continental, was dismissed for a broadcast that did not keep to the official line.

Propagandists were quick to seize on the sinking of the *Belgrano* as evidence of British 'savagery'. The Foreign Ministry sent an immediate cable to all embassies and consulates to capitalise on this tragic event. One story, widely circulated, was a comment allegedly made by a survivor: 'The first torpedo was war, the second was murder.' Even some British reporters picked up this story and related it as if it were true. In Brazil thirty million television viewers were told in the main news of the night on 30 April that the British had machine-gunned survivors of the *General Belgrano* in the water. This viciously false report emanated from Buenos Aires. On the same day Argentine news announced that a British air raid near Port Darwin had killed eleven of the islanders –

another false story, designed to frighten the Falklanders.

The Argentinian propagandists made enormous use of television. A frequently shown advertisement-like clip depicted a majestic lion – Great Britain – loping across the screen; it was followed by the sights of a telescopic rifle, from left to right across the screen – and *crack!* – the beast crashed to the ground. The aggressor in the Malvinas had paid for his insolence.

Another clip showed a Mirage fighter taking off and dipping its delta wing in salute as it set off on a bombing run. Yet another showed two young pilots in their respective cockpits talking over the radio to each other – 'Can you see any sign of la Thatcher's pirates?' All communiqués, direct from the joint chiefs of staff, were announced on television to the sound of martial music and on the screen flashed the Services symbol – the flame of liberty, with an anchor, a sword and a wing. The blue and white Argentinian flag, a great inspiration to most Argentinians, was shown every half hour, even mid-way through programmes.

The Peronists, the military's traditional opponents, were induced to make a public display in favour of holding on to the Malvinas. On 19 May a Peronist mass was held in Buenos Aires for those killed in battle. About 3,000 people filled the church and the Peronist leaders moved among them with their habitual hunched swagger. As the mass finished the crowd chanted 'Peron! Peron! We will triumph! We will return!' and then roamed the streets. The Junta leaders were constantly on hand to make impassioned speeches; Admiral Anaya was as colourful in his language as Galtieri. On Navy Day he said, 'The Navy is again in action. There could not be a more significant way to celebrate our navy's day. We are encouraged by the fresh memories of our dead which afflict our hearts and we renew our efforts to be victorious in a righteous cause. Our principles have been revitalised by our own blood and we stand up, proclaiming our truth and marching towards victory.' All three military leaders spoke eloquently of the sacrifices they were prepared to make – though not one of them had ever seen action.

The British were scrupulously correct in dealing with the prisoners they had taken in South Georgia, as the International Red Cross confirmed, but this did not prevent the Argentinian propagandists from inventing stories about torture. Indeed, the South Georgian 'heroes' became 'the tortured ones'. The battle for South Georgia, as reported in the Argentinian press on instructions from the Government, went on for at least two weeks; actually it was over in a matter of hours.

The Argentinians repeatedly understated their own losses and overstated the damage they had inflicted on the British. This is normal enough in war if only to mislead the enemy but the deception is effective only if the claims have some apparent credibility. Over the first weekend of May, for instance, the world was told that the British losses included eleven Harriers, two helicopters, one frigate badly damaged and three others damaged. At this point none of the claims was true except for slight splinter damage to one plane. Since it was known that the British had started with only twenty Harriers the situation was soon reached – by adding up the Argentinian claims – where the British had lost more aircraft than they left England with.

A mysterious item appeared on the front page of a Buenos Aires afternoon newspaper on 5 May. Headlined 'The Hermes Sunk?' the story said that according to the Soviet news agency Tass (how would Tass know?) the British aircraft carrier had been bombed and sunk. No official comment came from the Junta but in the international press room of the Sheraton Hotel an Air Force officer confided, 'We did it with a little Pucara plane that dropped six bombs and thirty-two rockets.' The Argentinian propaganda machine seemed peculiarly fascinated by the *Hermes*. In a government film shown on all television stations a raft and lifejackets imprinted *Hermes* 554 were shown abandoned on the shore of the Falklands; a commentator asked breathlessly, 'Is this a sign of the sinking of the *Hermes*?'

For many of the 750 journalists accredited at the Foreign Ministry in Buenos Aires since 2 April the one available personality was 'the Source'. It was to this person, who could not be named, that even the Government news agency, Telam, went to plant leaks and rumours. Telam had always been the single largest generator of rumour in Argentina because it had a monopoly on all government departments. Margot Hornblower of the *Washington Post* wrote about the difficulties and frustrations of not being able to get straightforward news, only the official version from 'the Source'. She met an American newsman who had solved the problem. 'Sometimes I just listen to the news from the B.B.C.,' he told her, tapping his shortwave radio affectionately, 'and I report it from Buenos Aires.'

The Junta accused Britain of not acknowledging its claims because of strict censorship imposed by Mrs Thatcher. In Buenos Aires the most frequently quoted Englishman was Tony Benn (Tooni Bin). Also a stream of extracts from the *Guardian* and a mixture of imprecations and equivocations from Dame Judith Hart reinforced the Junta's wish to believe that Britain did not have the stomach for serious sacrifices over the Falklands.

Argentine propaganda made great use of an article by John Pilger of the *Daily Mirror*, published in the *New York Times*. Pilger made the questionable assertion that many British people lamented that Britain had willingly surrendered its considerable political skills 'so that its leadership, bellicose in the extreme, can satiate a need to use force and glorify force'.

Time and again stories appeared claiming that the British warships were trapped; some newspapers, reporting the San Carlos landing – several days late – carried the government's assurance that none of the invading fleet would escape from Falkland Sound. The propagandists appeared to give no thought to the consequence when these and other stories would be proved false.

The Argentinians scored significant international propaganda success with their film of a young Argentine widow walking in grief behind the coffin of her sailor husband. She was pregnant and her lips were twisted as she wept. The scene was shown – and repeated on most British television networks over the weekend of 7–9 May. British journalists reporting the funeral said that the Argentinians claimed that eight of their sailors had been killed when their patrol boat was attacked by a British helicopter. They had been engaged in rescuing survivors from the sunken *General Belgrano* when they were attacked, according to the official story, 'with a treachery hitherto unknown in the history of war at sea.'

It made a good story, even if most of it was false. Only one sailor had died in the attack and the British had rescued the crew. It was typical of the propaganda coups which the Argentinians were able to get onto television screens all over the world. The film was also typical of the sympathetic coverage of Argentinian tragedies which angered Mrs Thatcher and many ordinary British people; there seemed to be no balance of British tragedies but the British, of course, could not compete in a contest of grief. They do not parade their sorrow and British corpses were far away in the Falklands.

One Telam communiqué which had wide international coverage was designed to show that Argentina was trying to make life as comfortable as possible for the Falkland islanders. It was part of a studied paternalistic approach calculated to impress on foreign journalists the notion that the Falklanders were part of the Argentinian family. 'Arrangements have been made to reinforce the professional staff at the local hospital; in addition to two British lady doctors working there previously three Argentinian doctors are now also there. Everything has been taken into account to ensure medical assistance to the local population ...' And there followed fabricated details about how the islanders were enjoying good and plentiful food.

But the Argentinians perpetrated a particularly clumsy piece of propaganda late in May when the Ministry of the Interior made a public display of issuing an Argentinian passport to a young British Falkland Islander. Just what inducement they offered this young, incoherent and gullible shepherd is not clear. With some reluctance his Argentinian sponsors allowed the foreign press to question him and his sincerity at once became questionable.

The Junta members and their officials appear to have lived in a fantasy world, repeatedly denying what even other Latin American countries knew to be true. The *Christian Science Monitor* said that Argentina was living in a state of national self-deception. Rumours were taken as fact provided that they were disseminated by the official media and the distortions and lies prevented any reasonable argument in the country. The Church lent its weight to the 'national self-deception'. A masterly coup was for Galtieri to induce the principal Argentinian cardinal to kiss him publicly – thus implying that the Church backed the war effort. This was a more subtle piece of propaganda than most.

Many Argentinian reports, one must conclude, were written wholly for internal consumption and in the knowledge that the foreign press – and most foreign governments – would treat them with derision. Sandy Woodward's suicide of despair and the bombing of the *Hermes* by Mirages in late April were examples of this type of propaganda.

News of the British landings brought stunned

disbelief at first because the public had been conditioned to believe that such a happening was impossible. When even the most bellicose optimists could see that Argentina just might lose the Malvinas the propagandists prepared the ground. The *Buenos Aires Herald*, an English language paper, ran a government-sponsored cartoon showing a champion boxer, assisted by a second champion wearing the Stars and Stripes, using dirty punches against a novice challenger. The caption read: 'Who can call it "losing" if the smalltown amateur is beaten by top-ranked heavyweights – especially if the young challenger's opponents go away with black eyes and broken noses?'

But with defeat staring Argentina in the face, as the British troops were preparing to take Port Stanley, the Junta and their propaganda machine had not even told the Argentinian people about their 250 dead at Goose Green and the 1,400 taken prisoner. The propaganda stories were still about non-existent Argentinian victories.

The homecoming of the *Belgrano* survivors to Buenos Aires and that of the *Sheffield* survivors to Brize Norton provided an interesting contrast in national attitudes. The Argentinian sailors arrived to an emotional, brass-band welcome and they were met by the President. They reaffirmed their pledge to die for their flag if necessary. The British sailors came home to a low-key family greeting and no fanfare; in Britain thinking to capitalise on such a private occasion would have been intolerable.

In Britain the handling of propaganda and information and its presentation by the Ministry of

Defence, the Services and the media was very different from Argentina. If some military leaders had been allowed their way there would have been a once-daily 'Official Communiqué', but Ministers insisted on better Press briefing arrangements. Even then it took the Defence Ministry about a month to establish an adequate system. (Press arrangements were better during the Suez crisis in 1956.)

Early in the campaign information seemed to be rationed. For instance, the Ministry issued a communiqué announcing that British helicopters had detected and attacked a hostile Argentine submarine 'in the vicinity' of South Georgia. This was all. The press needed to know if the helicopters had detected the submarine making a torpedo attack on British warships; had the British in turn attacked with torpedoes? had the submarine been sunk with all hands? was the attack carried out by Sea King anti-submarine aircraft? how had they detected the submarine? Only when the Argentinians announced that helicopters had machine-gunned a submarine on the surface at Grytviken did the real story come to light.

Few people at the Ministry seem to have understood, even by the end of May, that news management in 1982 is not just about censorship. Much of it is about supplying pictures, preferably movie films but still photographs rather than nothing at all. If television journalists had no British-originated pictures they either showed Argentine ones or sat people in front of the camera and invited them to speculate.

Why should photographs not have been sent of the

Port Stanley airfield after the bombing? The Argentinians certainly knew what it looked like. Photographs could have been sent of the task force without disclosing its location or anything else of value to the enemy. The press were not allowed to film or photograph the *Sheffield* until four days after she had been hit.

The Ministry seems to have worked to different rules from those observed by the censors on the ships of the fleet. The most extraordinary divergence between the Ministry and the fleet censors occurred over the bombing raid by Vulcans operating from Ascension Island. On the ships journalists were told that this was top secret, not just for the duration of the war but for years to come; it was almost in the category of 'never to be revealed'. Half an hour later the B.B.C. announced – from Ministry information – that Vulcans had flown from Ascension and bombed Port Stanley airfield.

Fleet officers frequently asked journalists not to include certain important military developments – but a few hours later censor and journalists would hear them over the B.B.C., courtesy of the Ministry of Defence. On the day H.M.S. *Sheffield* was hit by an Exocet journalists with the ships were told that C-in-C Fleet, London, had ordered an embargo on the news. A blackout was also applied to the loss of two Harriers in an accident in thick fog. But the details of both incidents were released to a press conference in London.

On *Hermes* copy was vetted by Roger Goodwin, a defence ministry press officer, the captain's secretary and finally by the captain himself. It was then transmitted to H.M.S. *Warrior* at Northwood, where somebody else censored the censored version. Michael Nicholson, in a complaint to I.T.N.'s editor, said, 'We were told this morning by the Admiral's staff aboard *Hermes* that there were no incidents to report overnight – poor visibility and no activity in the air. Minutes afterwards on the B.B.C. World Service we heard the Ministry of Defence spokesman announcing surface engagements off the Falklands and that the Task Force had fired on a vessel.'

Throughout the war the great bulk of the British press, supported, encouraged and at times incited the British Government. Seldom has editorial comment been so unequivocal. 'If Britain backs down the world is up for grabs,' Peregrine Worsthorne proclaimed in the *Sunday Telegraph*.

Yet in Parliament Mrs Thatcher stated that 'many people are very concerned indeed that the case for our British forces is not being heard fully and effectively' within the country. She was referring particularly to television. Her Government was certainly concerned that Britain was not adequately countering Argentinian propaganda and was displeased about the way the B.B.C. was handling its material; some Conservatives said that the B.B.C. was giving the impression of being pro-Argentine and anti-Britain.

This criticism was too sweeping but errors of judgment occurred. Soon after Britain declared the twelve-mile exclusion zone both B.B.C. and I.T.V. showed Argentine helicopter gunships patrolling the Falklands coastline – apparently in open defiance of Harrier patrols. Only later did commentators point out that they did not know when the film was taken –

or where; it might not have been in the Falklands at all.

On 9 May I.T.V.'s 'Weekend World' permitted the Argentine Defence Minister to explain at length how the spirit of the Argentinians was unquenched; he and the armed forces were ready to thrash the British. After the interview the presenter, Brian Walden, cautioned that viewers should take a lot of the minister's comments with 'a pinch of salt'. But the programme posed the question whether, in wartime, an enemy should be given such a prime opportunity to push propaganda.

Sometimes what appeared to be biased reporting or discussion was probably nothing more than an ill considered choice of words. Peter Snow, on the B.B.C., told the nation that *if we believed* British sources we had no casualties at all (this was before the sinking of the *Sheffield*). He did not mean to imply that he disbelieved the Ministry.

One difficulty for the media as Richard Francis, managing director of B.B.C. Radio, said on 11 May, was that ninety per cent of the facts about the Falklands seemed to be coming out of Argentina. The word 'facts' was an unfortunate choice but certainly Argentina was supplying a vast quantity of news.

British journalists were well aware that the propaganda-information war was being lost and they blamed the Ministry of Defence. The charge had substance. The Ministry was late firing its shots, its censorship was heavy and multilayered and it failed to provide adequate facilities for television pictures to be transmitted back to Britain from the war zone. The film of the compelling interview the B.B.C.'s Brian

Hanrahan had with Captain 'Sam' Salt after the sinking of the *Sheffield* took three weeks to reach London, long after any security considerations applied. In fact, no British films from South Georgia or the Falklands exclusion zone were seen for the first three weeks of hostilities.

The appointment of Mr Ian MacDonald as spokesman for the Ministry of Defence was a mistake. A likeable, civilised and sincere man, Mr MacDonald did not have the crisply confident and professional air needed in a spokesman. His slow-motion enunciation might have been helpful for journalists whose first language was not English but it frustrated others. He seemed to think he was addressing dullards. In any case, he was badly chosen to appear before millions of English television viewers; as he took his seat and prepared his melancholy features for his lugubrious voice one instinctively expected disaster. Even triumphs, such as the capture of Goose Green, were presented in tones of measured sepulchral solemnity. Mr MacDonald had a further handicap – the material which he was given to read was written in a flat, lifeless style.

Sometimes he met reporters' questions with replies of startling opacity. At one time a journalist asked him if British forces had tried to carry out helicopter landings on the Falklands as Argentina claimed. The reply: 'What I have said throughout to that kind of question is that interesting though it may be, I have throughout the whole of the last four weeks never made a comment on it but have always said that

I hope that no one will think my comment means more than quite simply no comment.'

British national propaganda should have been presented along the lines of the outraged citizen defending his own property. It should have asked peoples of other countries to put themselves in the British position and it could have made more use of stories about the Falklanders themselves. I know of United Nations diplomats who did not know that the Falklanders' natural language is English. Again, it was left to the British press to present the Falklanders' case, and to tell the world about their British way of life. For instance, the few police in the Falklands dress as British bobbies; this interesting and significant fact appears to have been noted by only one publication – *Woman's Own*.

Official information services made little use of the Governor, Rex Hunt, though this articulate man knew more about the Falklanders' feelings than did anybody else. A human-interest story about Mr Hunt in the *Daily Mail* showed what might have been achieved had he been used in official propaganda.

The British also failed to stress the barbarous nature of the Argentinian regime; even Ministers rarely referred to the torture and murder of thousands of Argentinians, a fact which must discredit the Argentinian leaders and their claim that they would bring humane government to the occupied Falkland Islands. It was left to the British press to stress the cruelties of the fascist government. Similarly, even though it was known by the end of April that General Menendez was holding Falkland

Islanders in prison conditions, the British made no capital out of this information.

Again, British Ministries failed to stress that Britain is the greatest *de*colonising nation history has known. Francis Pym made this point in an interview with a South American journalist but it should have been given wide publicity throughout the Third World. One theme begged to be exploited. Why, in the name of reason, should Britain be interested in colonising the Falkland Islands? Since reports of mineral riches were nothing more than the wildest speculation, the truth was that Britain went to immense trouble and expense to fight a war in the South Atlantic purely because of its concern for the freedom of an independent people. Mrs Thatcher several times made this point but it was not taken up and widely disseminated, as it should have been.

Charles Wheeler, at the UN for the B.B.C., was aware of propaganda failings. He commented one evening that the diplomats were not hearing enough about the support of British *opposition* leaders for the Government's determination to free the Falklands from occupation. The official attitude of many countries would have been influenced by this simple fact. That supremely able diplomat, Sir Anthony Parsons, could have made more of the unity among British politicians on the point of no negotiation before Argentinian withdrawal; in fact, even the freak fringe led by Mr Benn appeared to go that far with the Government.

Some British newspapers did themselves no credit – and gave the Argentinians fuel for their propaganda machine – with crude headlines. When the *Belgrano* was sunk *The Sun* splashed across its front page one word – GOTCHA. *The Sun* also sponsored a missile to be fired by one of the planes in the task force. Its reporter wrote, 'Up yours, Galtieri' on the missile. And the paper ran a series of jingoistic headlines, the most memorable – or deplorable – over a story about a British rejection of Argentinian settlement ideas – 'Stick it up your Junta'.

Other headlines from the tabloids included 'Give 'Em Hell' and 'In We Go'. The *News of the World* cheapened the war to a sporting event, with the shouting headline 'Latest Score: Britain 6 Argentina Zero'.

Calculated leaks to the foreign press have long been a war technique used by British ministries and there were some classic examples during the Falklands war. The most notable concerned the nuclear submarine *Superb*; the Ministry of Defence encouraged speculation that the deadly submarine was in the South Atlantic in early April. It was not but the story had the effect of keeping the Argentine Navy in port.

On other occasions the Ministry contributed to the enemy's Intelligence. It announced, for instance, that some enemy bombs were not exploding. The first disclosure came on 13–14 May when the Ministry revealed that a bomb had gone clean through a frigate. Then came the disclosure about the successful defusing of two bombs on H.M.S. *Antrim*. Within days both the *Antelope* and the *Coventry* were lost in bombing attacks. As I have already described, in the *Antelope*'s case the bomb disposal expert was unable to defuse the bomb and was killed. It may have been a coincidence that the Skyhawks appeared to have changed the height of their bombing runs and some experts on the spot thought the Argentinians may have altered bomb fuse settings.

The Ministry's disclosures should certainly have caused the Argentinian high command to find out at once why bombs were not exploding; such knowledge would prevent a repetition. It was not in the British interest to bring about such an inquiry; the Ministry should have allowed the Argentinians to believe that the bombs had missed.

The Ministry – and the B.B.C. World Service – were guilty of negligence in announcing that the 2nd Parachute Battalion's raid on Goose Green had occurred before it had even started. It is not possible to know if this alerted the defenders but it might have done.

The media, particularly television, was most at fault in giving information and ideas to the Argentinians. I doubt if this was ever done deliberately; ignorance, naivety and thoughtlessness were to blame. Day after day television produced batteries of retired admirals, generals and air marshals to pronounce on the conflict: 'What would you do, General, if you were the Argentinian commander (or the British commander?)' 'How would you make it more difficult for the Argentine planes to reach our ships?' 'If you were planning an attack on Port Stanley what thoughts would be in your mind?'

The senior officers, apparently with no more sense of security than the interviewer, gave insights into British military thinking, listed the options open to commanders on both sides, and discussed the weapons available to them. On one occasion an admiral showed on a large map just where he thought the British fleet would be at that moment. Videotapes of these programmes were en route to Buenos Aires within hours. Just how useful they really were to Argentine Intelligence we will never know, but they could have been very helpful had the Argentinians been skilful enough to interpret the information so freely handed to them. If General Menendez did not know the likely tactics to be used against him it was not the fault of British television.

Newspapers were less frequently at fault although one incident horrified me. The newspaper concerned, generally responsible in what it printed, suggested a way in which the Argentinians could sink a British ship, even an aircraft carrier. Because it was a fully practical idea I cannot repeat it here, or even give the paper's name; if the Argentinians were to go to war again they could use the plan presented to them.

Certainly much of the information given on television and radio, and in newspapers, is available to anybody who subscribes to defence and armaments journals. But what is not so generally available is British military thinking; the generals, admirals and air marshals provided the Argentinians with plenty of that.

While the press in general supported Mrs Thatcher and the government, the *Guardian* – and to a lesser extent the *Financial Times* – was consistent in its opposition. Some comments from the *Guardian*'s political columnist Peter Jenkins sum up the paper's attitude.

159

'It is a war quite disproportionate to the principles held to be at stake. It is a war brought about by aggression and intransigence of a military dictatorship and the negligence and self-delusion of a once imperial power. It will neither save nor serve the world. It is a war not worth fighting, no more than it was when the fleet set sail from Portsmouth. It is a war made immoral by its futility.' 12 May.

'... When it comes to intransigence there is not much to choose between a Thatcher and a Galtieri... The world may be excused if it sees two nations in need of war, each struggling to escape from a spiral of decline and in need of heroic respite ... The Establishment ... goes into this war with an uneasy conscience. There is an awful feeling that it has been too serious a business to have been left to Margaret Thatcher.' 30 May.

Because the B.B.C. External Services in Spanish were being jammed there was little which Britain could do to counteract the effect of the Argentinian propaganda within Argentina. At least the jamming indicated that the B.B.C. radio's objective and impartial coverage of the Falklands affair was reaching a larger audience in Argentina than the Argentinian authorities would like.

But the Foreign Office could have made more use of ridicule to expose the falsity of Argentinian claims, just as they could have stressed, in dignified terms, that the British are never guilty of such barbarities as machine-gunning survivors in the water.

In some ways the Foreign Office was highly efficient, notably after the failure of negotiations to produce a peaceful settlement. Every embassy and

British Prime Minister Margaret Thatcher meets with Falkland Governor Rex Hunt after his return from the islands following the Argentine invasion.

An Argentine soldier practices hand-to-hand combat.

Right: Members of A Company, Royal Marine Commandos, exercise on the deck of HMS *Hermes* as she heads toward the South Atlantic and the Falklands.

Below: Royal Marines line up for a weapons check in à hangar aboard HMS *Hermes*, the flagship of the British Islands task force.

Top: The Argentine cruiser *General Belgrano* lists heavily as it begans to sink after being attacked by a British submarine. 368 Argentine sailors were lost.

Bottom: Smoke pours from the British destroyer HMS *Sheffield* after the ship is hit by a missile. It later sank, taking with it twenty of the ship's crew.

Right: Captured Argentine soldiers being guarded by a Royal Marine as they await transit out of Goose Green.

Below: The HMS *Antelope* explodes in flame in Carlos Bay off the East Falklands after an Argentine bomb, lodged in the ship's engine room, detonates.

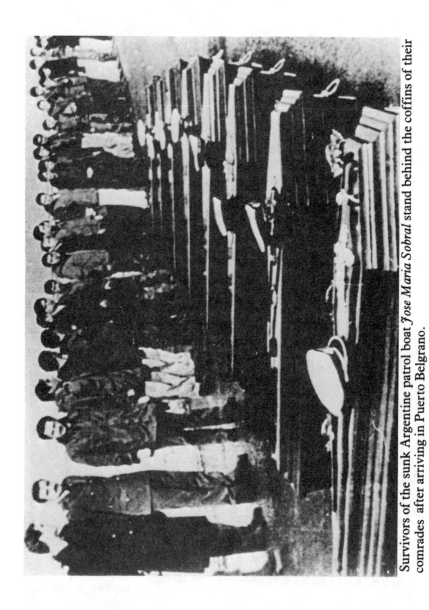

Survivors of the sunk Argentine patrol boat *Jose Maria Sobral* stand behind the coffins of their comrades after arriving in Puerto Belgrano.

Returning with 2,500 Royal Marines, the luxury liner *Canberra*, nicknamed "The Great White Whale," returned unscathed to a riotous welcome in Southampton, England.

The Union Jack and White Ensign flags are raised on South Georgia after the island's recapture by the British.

consulate was sent an explanation of the entire proceedings so that they could better explain to foreign politicians that the British had negotiated in good faith and had made major concessions to meet the Argentinians' demands.

Perhaps not surprisingly the Soviet was a victor in the propaganda war. It made the most of the opportunity to label Britain a 'stubborn colonialist' and to brand the United States as a 'betrayer of the nations it had pretended to befriend' – the Latin American countries. The Soviet leaders had been trying for some years to get a foothold in South America and they saw the collapse of the United States' prestige as their opportunity. *Pravda* said that 'the restoration of the colonial status of the Falklands is out of the question'. And Soviet leaders either directly or through their controlled press asked the world to notice that Britain, one of the senior partners in NATO, was still bent on 'stealing territory and rebuilding its old empire'.

The propaganda war which proceeded in parallel with the South Atlantic shooting war showed, above all, that control of the media could never again be as it was during World War I and World War II. Just as new weapons had appeared so too had new relationships. In future the government and the media will need to make allowances for each other's needs, in the national interest; military security and public information must be balanced.

Above all, the British government needs information officers who understand the speed with which news reports are flashed across the world; that is, officers with knowledge of electronic news-gathering and the sending of reports by satellite. News now travels so fast that each side in a conflict needs to get its version of events in front of the public before the other side does. In the Falklands war the British official information distributors appeared to have no conception of this principle.

Had the Government's information services been more professionally prepared for the war they might have avoided the damaging criticisms made by John Pilger and published in the *New York Times*. Pilger's final sentence reads, 'It is clear that the government, through the Ministry of Defence, decided at the start to prevent the war from being reported as war.'

This is demonstrably not so. In permitting so many journalists to accompany the task force the Government was not able to prevent the war being reported as war, even if it wanted to, but information ineptitude gave Pilger and others an opening for their allegations. But the Ministry made a major error of judgment in not permitting at least some foreign journalists to accompany the expedition; not a single non-British reporter went. Inevitably, this led to the belief, however erroneous, that the British Government could have the war reported on terms favourable to itself. In fact, it would have been advantageous to Britain to have had independent American, German and French journalists and cameramen – and perhaps others – with the task force; they could have told their own public, in their own way, about the British effort, and they could have corroborated British accounts of the various actions. In short, by not taking aboard foreign-language correspondents the Ministry was denying

Britain an information advantage.

The twenty-two war correspondents who went to the war did an excellent job under difficult and dangerous conditions, imposed by the nature of the war itself, the weather and the Ministry of Defence. That some produced better stories than others was largely a matter of luck; those stuck on remote ships had no chance to get great stories. The work of Robert Fox, B.B.C., Michael Nicholson, I.T.N., and Max Standish, *Evening Standard* was particularly memorable. Correspondents never claim any heroism for themselves but those in the Falklands often risked their lives to get the stories the British people read in safety at home.

Politicians made allegations that there were traitors in the B.B.C. and I.T.V.; officers in the South Atlantic asked angrily if they had to fight the Ministry of Defence and the B.B.C. as well as the Argentinians; war correspondents complained of censors who made life difficult; and some journalists upbraided other journalists for betraying national values.

There were no traitors. The B.B.C., I.T.V., the Ministry, the censors and the media – even the *Guardian* – performed as their personal and professional conscience demanded. In a democracy where everybody may have his say there are bound to be dissenting voices. Dissent did not dissipate the national will during what the *Sunday Times* called 'The war that had to be'. But it was a war won without the information services of the Ministry of Defence; they came into the action almost too late.

11 Costs and Consequences

Before making his decision to visit Britain in May 1982 Pope John consulted Cardinal Basil Hume about the result of a Gallup poll on British attitudes to the visit, a fact which *The Times* considered 'almost shocking'.

Did Jesus Christ consult Gallup polls before riding into Jerusalem?' *The Times* asked, implying that the Pope should be above the findings of opinion polls – and of political animosities, in this case the British-Argentine dispute.

His constant references to the Falklands war while he was in Britain, and to the suffering and death it caused, perhaps made people everywhere a little more conscious of the evil of war in general. The Pope's increasingly political role was shown up to a startling degree as a consequence of the British-Argentine dispute. That he felt it necessary to make a special trip to Argentina may have shown that he was not taking sides; it certainly showed that he takes political factors into account. The British Government made no attempt to exploit the Pope's visit politically but it was only to be expected that the Argentinians would. The propaganda line was: 'The Pope visited Britain as a commitment; he came to Argentina from love.' Galtieri's attempts to be 'close' to the Pope were surprisingly successful for a supposedly non-political visit.

The Pope might not have been taking sides but the Archbishop of Canterbury, Dr Runcie, did. Preaching on 23 May he said that had Britain turned the other cheek to the Falkland Islands invaders, 'We should have been accomplices in making the world an even less stable place . . . We are using armed force to reverse an invasion and to baulk the attempt to decide the future of the Falkland Islands by aggression and the use of military power.' The churches generally made pronouncements on 'the South Atlantic crisis' – as most of them persisted in calling it. Few of the Church statements had a distinctly religious dimension. Like it or not churchmen were finding themselves in contemporary politics to a degree that did not exist even during World War II. After the British-Argentine conflict church isolationism will never be quite the same again.

While the Pope and the Archbishop were concerned more than anything else about the suffering and loss of life, others, more materialistic – and militaristic – were making cost-effectiveness computer studies of the costs of future wars, the way they might be fought, and the changes that would be necessary to armaments and material in the light of the Falklands war.

For Argentina, the cost of the war was so ruinous that U.S. State Department analysts concluded that spending on the Falklands war might stop the country from ever having a first-class economy. The cost of 'repelling the British invader', as the Argentinian Minister of the Economy expressed it, was £16 million a month. This figure is suspect; U.S. Government economists reported to the State Department that between 2 April and 20 May Argentina had spent £700 million in direct military costs.

With foreign exchange reserves of only £2 billion Argentina was faced with a bill in 1982 of nearly £4 billion in repayments and interest on foreign debt. This meant that the country needed to seek 'roll-over' agreements with its foreign creditors, among them British and American banks. A default on Argentina's debt would send a massive shock wave through the international financial community, so Western bankers would have no choice but to re-schedule the outstanding loans. Military replacement costs will run to several hundred million pounds, the largest bill being for new aircraft. In the air or on the ground the British had destroyed eighty-three Argentinian planes. With inflation at 150 per cent the Argentinians will never be out of debt.

In Britain the government was prepared for an expensive war – though in the end it was much less expensive than anticipated. Sir Terence Lewin warned the War cabinet that losses in the initial stages of a landing might amount to a quarter of the naval force.

Defence Minister Nott told the House of Commons that money was an irrelevance in the retaking of the Falklands and most members cheered him. When hostilities commenced his ministry had estimated the likely cost of the war to be £250 million, over and above the wages and other costs which would have been met even if the task force had not sailed, but excluding replacement costs. By the end of May the revised figure was £500 million but it was more likely to be £1 billion. The costs were manageable but they made a sizeable dent in the Defence Contingency Fund of £2.2 billion. In any case the expense was largely absorbed by the £12 billion defence budget.

The expense of maintaining the 8,000-mile logistics line was about £3 million a day until the counter invasion of East Falkland, when it rose to about £5 million a day. The largest amount was the cost of the chartered and requisitioned ships – £18 million a week in June. Fuel, at 65p a gallon, cost about £3 million a week; twenty-five million gallons were used between 2 April and 12 May.

The *Canberra* payments included a £750,000 requisition fee for thirty days and £450,000 for the *Uganda*; this was in addition to the weekly fees. Because of the glut in the tanker market the Government was readily able to charter the fourteen tankers, eight of which were from BP, who were paid forty per cent above the normal tanker rate because of the hazards of the mission.

Insurance cover for the civilian ships and crews was also a charge for the government. P and O, the owners of the *Canberra, Uganda* and two roll-on roll-off ferries, argued that its share of the highly competitive cruise and passenger ferry market could be seriously damaged by taking the ships out of service; the company would need to be compensated for this. Government officials and shipping operators negotiated almost daily to establish the Government's liability for loss of earnings, re-establishing the ships in the competitive cruise market and the cost of making good any damage and the military conversion work, such as the helicopter pads. Thousands of square metres of chipboard were laid in the *QE2* to protect carpets, no small item.

No matter what the final figure, the cost of the Falklands war did not disturb the national economy, but the implication for long term defence spending was profound. The estimates of 1981 were for £12.3 billion, with a government commitment to increase spending, in real terms, by three per cent until 1985. Even before the Falklands affair Service chiefs were competing for the additional £1 billion. In addition, there would need to be a complex upgrading of weapons systems to take the lessons of the Falklands into account. And the Government probably could not now afford to make economies by closing the Royal dockyards at Portsmouth and Chatham.

The costs of all war will increase enormously as a result of the Falklands war because armaments manufacturers realise that there will be an even greater demand for missiles, counter missiles and protection against missiles. Soon after an Exocet destroyed the *Sheffield*, Libya was offering £500,000 on the black market for any Exocet. France had by then sold 271 Exocets to equip seventy-six planes in seven countries.

The Russians were particularly interested in the destructive power of Exocets. As long ago as 1971 they converted several destroyers to carry the SS-N-2c, a sea-skimming missile with a range of fifty miles, and the Russian 'Charlie' class submarines which first entered service in 1967 have the SS-N-7, a sea-skimmer with a range of thirty-three miles. In addition Soviet long-range naval aircraft since about 1975 have had the 'Kitchen' anti-ship missile, with a range of between 190 and 500 miles which is designed to approach a ship below radar detection level. The only British weapon with a capability comparable to the Exocet is the Sea Eagle, not yet in service, which will be used from Sea Harriers and R.A.F. Buccaneers.

But the high effectiveness of the Sea Wolf short-range missile and associated radar system against fast, low-incoming aircraft was proved. Much was also learned about the operational use of the Sea Dart higher-level missile system and about the decoying of incoming Argentine missiles. The success of the handheld Blowpipe missile, which can be carried and fired by one man and brought into action in five seconds, will inspire more research into similar weapons.

As a result of the war the sales of arms by the principal Western manufacturers – the U.S., Britain, France, West Germany and Italy – will need to be considered. Arms sellers have always sought to gain political advantage in return for arms, but as the Americans discovered in Iran and the Russians in Egypt, China and Somalia, alliances made on such terms are unstable. With so many countries selling to so many buyers it is not possible to predict against whom a weapon will be fired. The French would not have expected that Argentina would be using Exocets against Britain. In any case some buyers, such as Libya, are prepared to resell to other nations. It was bitter irony that Argentina used British-built ships, aeroplanes and weapons against the British forces.

Much of the thinking about how ships should be defended will be revised. Some ships were found to be too lightly armed, others are prone to damage from fire especially if they have a high aluminium content. Aluminium began to displace steel plate for warship superstructure – everything above the hull – after World War II. Its lightness helped stability as masts, equipment and weapons grew higher on the upper decks. The eight Type 21 frigates built for the Royal Navy contain 750 tons of steel and 120 tons of aluminium. The experience of the *Sheffield* shows that aluminium quickly melts and sets fire to electricity cabling and other vital equipment.

The lessons gained for the future for British defence systems, tactics, ship design and offensive missile design are incalculable. Flexibility will be the key word for the military planners and designers; ships will need to be multi-purpose – just as the Harrier was shown to be. Ships' fire-fighting and damage-control systems must be re-assessed and modified.

The war had its political, strategic and tactical lessons as well. The entire operation gave the Soviet Union an entirely new perception of Western political will. The quick decision to send the task force in itself and then the bombing of the Port Stanley airfield was a demonstration of political incisiveness which is known to have impressed the Soviet leadership. NATO diplomats said that the British response to Argentina's challenge was a 'useful reminder' to the Russians that the West will, if necessary, use force to deter aggression.

The British experience was envied by both

Americans and Russians; the last American amphibious landing took place at Inchon, in September 1950, during the Korean War. The speed with which the task force was assembled, the merchant ships taken over and converted and the 100,000 different military items assembled astonished senior American naval officers; some told me an operation on this scale would have taken the U.S. three months. If it impressed the Americans it will have made the Russians thoughtful. The Russians were interested in the South Atlantic operations from the beginning; they had two information gathering satellites over the area two days *before* the Argentinians invaded the Falklands. The staff at the Russian Embassy doubled by the end of May and by mid-June an estimated thirty Russian 'advisers' had arrived.

Britain's place in Europe became more secure after the Falklands affair because of European respect for the British action. 'Would Heath have done what Margaret Thatcher is doing?' Chancellor Schmidt is reported to have asked President Mitterand after the fleet sailed. 'Nobody since Eden would have done it,' Mitterand replied. Not that he was seeking to find a parallel with Suez. Parallels exist but not in the essentials. The background is not one of secret and sinister plotting but incompetence in Whitehall; the cause with the Falklands was a just one, unlike the Suez 'cause'; with Suez the military response was timid, in the Falklands it was positive and unequivocal; in 1956 Eden was hamstrung by Eisenhower but in 1982 Thatcher was supported by Reagan.

A parallel would develop if Mrs Thatcher were to accept U.N. trusteeship or other intervention in the Falklands, as a U.N. peace-keeping force was accepted in Lebanon, Sinai (between 1956-1967) and Cyprus. This would be the thin end of the wedge towards handing the islands over to Argentina and the beginning of a long period of uncertainty about sovereignty. It would also imply that Britain was ready to make concessions about territory its servicemen had died to liberate.

One British domestic parallel with Suez was evident from the beginning. It lay in the attitude of the Opposition. When Nasser seized the Suez Canal in 1956 Hugh Gaitskill, the Labour leader, attacked him and compared his actions with those of Hitler and Mussolini. When it became clear that the Government was preparing to use force Gaitskill reversed his support for Anthony Eden and began to insist that nothing should be done without the agreement of the United Nations. Within a few weeks the Opposition showed, through its parliamentary tactics, that it was no longer supporting a bipartisan approach. In 1982 Michael Foot vehemently supported action against Galtieri, even taking part in the arousal of public opinion towards military action. Then he slid sideways, urging negotiations and still more negotiations. His deputy Denis Healey asked questions which, intentional or not, tended to undermine confidence in the Government.

The Sunday Times considered that the Falklands affair would appear in history as a text book example of what can happen 'when nations refuse to foresee and act upon manifest dangers posed by an historical anomaly'. Margaret Thatcher had not known of the danger from Argentina but once she saw it she responded with celerity, as President Kennedy did at the time of the Soviet missiles in the Cuba crisis of 1963. The lesson of the Falklands affair is obvious: When caught wrong-footed, jump.

Mrs Thatcher showed that a woman can lead a European nation in war. Throughout the Falklands war her service chiefs appreciated her military virtue of clarity. Early in her Government this clarity had confused them because it was an unfamiliar quality in a politician. Soldiers in the South Atlantic certainly seemed to trust her, perhaps for the same reason. Some called her 'Mighty Maggie' which the Prime Minister probably preferred to 'Wonder Woman', a label affixed to her, with abusive intent, by Argentina's *Tal Cual*.

Never before has a British Government so taken the British public into its confidence about an aspect of foreign policy. This is partly because of Margaret Thatcher's commitment to open government; perhaps, more deeply, it indicates a trend towards the recognition that the public provides the money and the men to fulfil foreign policy. No British prime minister before Mrs Thatcher 'consulted' the people – through parliament, opinion polls and press – about the possibility of having to go to war. Mrs Thatcher did not say to the people in as many words, 'Well, what do you think?' But she was sensitive to their attitudes and she carried them with her. The dissenting voices were strident but not numerous. Most people seemed to be aware that Britain was standing alone in a just cause, even a noble one.

Newspapers reported that their volume of correspondence increased enormously because of the Falklands dispute; *The Times* received double its average 1,200 letters a week. An analysis of many hundreds of letters to a score of British publications showed about a two-thirds majority in favour of Mrs Thatcher's policy and actions. As many writers defended the B.B.C.'s coverage of the war as attacked it. Few letters, apart from those which suggested ways in which the conflict could be resolved, were without distress or anger or pride.

A Rhodes scholar professor working in Canada told the *Guardian* that 'The fleet is sailing forth like a bunch of drunks pouring out of a gaudy night ... What *am* I to tell my students now? That Britain is out fighting a lilliputian battle in the South Seas because she is seething with impotent rage?'

A *Daily Telegraph* reader could have suggested what the professor might tell his students. 'Freedom! What a wonderful word and how much more wonderful to enjoy it as we do ... There are those among us who say, "Bring back the fleet, don't fight." Let those who are free to air these views think back to when we were all saved by the actions of the Royal Air Force and the Battle of Britain. Did these dissenters cry out then "Stop the Air Force, ground the planes?" ... God bless our fleet and protect it in its endeavours.'

Mr John Doxat, in a letter to the *Daily Telegraph*, expressed the feelings of many. 'Why do we seem so obsessed with "international opinion"? Successful countries do not give a damn what the world thinks ... Kowtowing to "world opinion" gains no respect.

When Britain was truly powerful we were not liked, we were admired ... It is only by exercise of strength, in protection of our own, that we shall retain some of our prestige and regain a little of our greatness.'

Mr Peter Jay, through the *Times*, urged the Prime Minister to 'stand on the firm ground of the applicable principles, of the resolution of the British public and of the professionalism of the Royal Navy. Let not her fear the sophisticates on the other side of Downing Street, in Fleet Street and in Lime Grove. Let her ensure, rather, that desperadoes in Buenos Aires fear her.'

Certain phrases and concepts occurred many times. The anti-war anti-Thatcher camp used *jingoism, over-reaction, inflexible, when will they ever learn?; patriotism is the last refuge of a scoundrel, foolhardiness* (sending the fleet), *irrational; English chauvinism, colonialist tyrants, I renounce my British nationality forthwith.*

The anti-aggressor anti-Galtieri camp used *foolhardiness* (in invading the Falklands), *inflexible, when will they ever learn?, irrational, Argy macho, patriotic self-delusion, fascist brutes, the Junta has taken away the right of Argentina to be considered civilised.*

Despite support from those countries which imposed trade sanctions against Argentina, from New Zealand which lent a frigate to free another Royal Navy warship for the war zone, moral encouragement from Australia and some limited logistical support from the United States, Britain took the risks and fought alone. A seriously conducted opinion poll taken at the time of the British liberation invasion showed that the two most popular women in the world were Jane Fonda and Margaret Thatcher. Falkland Islanders, freed from a month's incarceration at Goose Green, sent a telegram to thank her for being 'steadfast'. Historians might well look back on the British-Argentine war as Margaret Thatcher's finest hour.

Not all commentators were able to appreciate Mrs Thatcher as a war leader. Bernard Crick, writing in the *New Statesman* of 14 May, thought that Britain's reaction to Galtieri's initial action was 'disproportionate'. He wrote: 'From the first dispatch of Mrs Thatcher's armada, one cannot get around the gross lack of proportion between means and ends . . . There has been a confusing multiplicity of aims and certainly a lack of proportion between the effects intended and the result achieved.' And he objected to military action having been launched before economic and diplomatic means were exhausted.

True, it had been launched but there had to be a lapse of at least three weeks before any action could be taken, and even longer before *land* action could be contemplated; there was time enough for diplomatic means to be tested. Economic sanctions against aggressor nations have never been effective, no matter how long they were in operation. When the fleet left Britain nobody could be sure what strength the expedition would need but many military experts thought they would be inadequate, not 'disproportionately high'. As for 'multiplicity of aims', there was only one aim – the single, non-negotiable purpose to get the Argentinians off the islands. No multiplicity of aims could have developed; compared with the task of achieving peace in the Middle East or bringing about arms limitations, the Falklands affair was a simple, straightforward dispute.

Mrs Thatcher's commanders in the field performed well. Admiral Woodward even violated a long-standing rule of war – and got away with it. He went against the teaching that has been driven into the minds of British naval commanders since 1940 – that air superiority is essential. Woodward would certainly have been taught about the disaster in Norway in 1940 when the *Luftwaffe* sank four British ships and badly damaged eighteen, including a carrier and a battleship. That expeditionary force, like the one of 1982, was hurriedly assembled and had to endure winter conditions. The troops who were landed were badly mauled and forced to withdraw. Woodward's calculated risk in landing without air superiority says much for the effectiveness of the Harrier vertical take-off aircraft, for the detailed planning and organisation behind the task force and about the skill and courage of the fighting men involved. To land 5,000 men, and reinforcements later, without losing a soldier to enemy action was remarkable. The first such loss was at Bluff Cove.

The day after the end of Operation Corporate – the Defence Ministry's secret codeword for the Falklands war – Major-General Moore nominated Brigadier Julian Thompson as 'man of the match'. It was a generous and well-deserved compliment. Thompson's driving leadership and tactical talent were evident from the moment the British landed on the shores of Port San Carlos, just as his imagination had been noticeable in the Pebble Island raid. Thompson is an associate member of the Gallipoli

Association; it is tempting to speculate that he learnt at least a little from studying the appalling mistakes made during the Gallipoli campaign of 1915, for he certainly made no mistakes of his own. The Falklands campaign was a superbly efficient military operation.

During the prelude to war and throughout the hostilities there was much talk of 'minimum force'. Following the Falklands campaign, politicians and people will need to be taught that the concept is meaningless. 'Minimum force' really means a hold-back war or a quasi war; quasi wars produce a quasi victory for one side and a quasi defeat for the other. This merely sets the scene for another round when the vanquished side has built up its strength. One of the basic principles of war is the use of *maximum* force; it will certainly be used by the Soviet should it decide to attack the United States or the West in general. A minimum response would then be suicide. Maximum force, which produces great damage and inflicts many casualties to bring about a quick defensive victory, might prevent the even more bloody attrition of a long war. Minimum force is a military irrelevance, whatever may be said for it in the moral and humane sense. Britain won back the Falklands because its leaders were prepared to hit hard, thus reducing British casualties. The Argentinians certainly had no intention of using minimum force to retain the islands, as its air force showed.

For the future the most serious warning for Britain presented by the conflict is that diplomatic intelligence must be of high quality. Most Western nations place much stress on military intelligence.

But intention of military attack is always preceeded by political signals; wars and revolutions have a gestation period, they do not just break out. The Iranian revolution was signalling itself twelve months before it occurred. The Falklands war will be presented by history as a classic example of a war that need not have happened.

Britain, as a NATO front-runner, needs an intellectual early warning system – formed not by civil servants (who almost by definition have no perception), not by the service chiefs (who are not sensitive to political alarm signals) and not professional intelligence agents (who are so busy concealing themselves that they sometimes do not see what they are looking at). The Prime Minister – any prime minister – needs a small First Appreciation Sensor Team (FAST?), made up of well-informed, much travelled men and women whose knowledge would be invaluable in predicting dangers from abroad threatening Britain politically, economically and militarily.

While much can be learnt from the Falklands war the situation itself was unique and will not be repeated elsewhere. The few remaining fragments of empire are either not the subject of territorial dispute (who would want St Helena?) or they are indefensible (as is Belize); or impregnable (Gibraltar); or left to Britain to govern by grace and favour (Hong Kong). The fleet cannot be rebuilt around the need to remain in the South Atlantic because Britain's real responsibility will remain in the North Atlantic and Western Europe – with the protection of Britain from air attack, security of supply routes and communications to the British Isles themselves and aid to Western Europe in the event of invasion.

Nevertheless, Britain's traditional strength lies in the kind of operation it undertook in the South Atlantic. This demands an effective capacity for maritime operations, which in turn demands a strong and diverse fleet, with a strong element of hunter-killer submarines. As a deterrent they are virtually unequalled; what Navy will put to sea if its ports are blockaded by hunter-killer submarines? In the army the emphasis must be on mobile and highly trained troops. The effectiveness of such soldiers in the battle for the Falklands will not be lost upon the countries of the Warsaw Pact.

Few expeditionary forces have faced such difficult problems of command and control, with its units scattered for much of the time over thousands of square miles of sea. The supreme commander, Woodward, used helicopters to bring his subordinates to him in *Hermes* for important conferences but there was no way of producing any real unity of command; army units, marines and support services were distributed among the ships. This dispersal makes all the more remarkable the achievement of landing an integrated force at Port San Carlos, with the many sub-units ready to co-operate with the field commander (Brigadier Thompson), whom most had not by then even seen. The chain of command, only basically in existence in Britain, was developed at sea and worked efficiently on land.

Without an expert war management staff Admiral Woodward, Major-General Moore and Brigadier Thompson could never have achieved what they did in the Falklands. It is more than ever clear that the security of Britain and the armed forces' ability to act rapidly demands a corps of 'war managers'. Their role in the implementation of foreign policy will be as important as those of the generals in the field.

Something must be said about Secretary of State Haig's request to Mrs Thatcher to be 'magnanimous in victory'. Other powerful voices urged that Argentina be left with some of its honour and that it not be wholly humiliated. The purpose of magnanimity was to avoid making the Argentinians bitterly resentful. But it could have the opposite effect; in Argentinian eyes a total defeat was more acceptable than one in which the victor deigned to be generous. Being permitted to keep the colours is usually a greater blow to pride than being forced to lower them. Apart from this most Latin American leaders in this situation would later rationalise that they were not really beaten; they had merely allowed the enemy to think that he had won. While there is no point in humiliating an enemy – it can rankle for years afterwards – being magnanimous has its dangers too; not the least of them is that it is never understood or tolerated by the men who have achieved the victory in the field.

Argentine national pride and honour will clamour for satisfaction; propaganda will present the British as invaders and aggressors and many senior army, navy and air force figures will want to embark on a long-term programme of bombings and torpedoing, if only to show that they could have succeeded where Galtieri, Anaya and Dozo failed.

They could be forestalled by a solution which is

practicable and, from the British and American point of view, desirable. Britain would retain sovereignty and the Americans would build a base on the Falklands thus furthering American geopolitical ambitions in the South Atlantic. The presence of this base would deter any Argentinian attack. Countries in Latin America – Cuba and Panama – have learnt to live with American bases on their territory and already America uses and pays for two British islands – Ascension in the Atlantic and Diego Garcia in the Indian Ocean. The Americans saw the need for a South Atlantic base several years ago and now might be the time to satisfy that need. The Latin Americans might protest and the Argentinians would be vociferous in their denunciation of America but u.s.-Argentine relations could hardly be worse than they were during the war. The islanders also might not like the idea but having been pitchforked out of the nineteenth century they cannot go back to it. Their 'paramount wishes' – to use a phrase much quoted during the negotiations – cannot be allowed to dominate the policies of the great nations trying to protect them.

If the Americans are not interested the alternative is for Britain to garrison the islands itself – with a combined operations force – at a cost of about £120 million a year – an estimate arrived at by comparing the requirements in the Falklands with those in Belize, where the cost is £4.5 million a year. At £120 million a year the burden would be light, though the initial establishment cost could be as much as £300 million.

The Falklands, together with the Falklands

dependencies, St Helena and Ascension Island could be integrated into the United Kingdom. As the task force showed, the Falklands are not as remote as most people had imagined.

12 Negotiations on Record

Earlier in the book I mentioned the plan of December 1980 put forward as a way to solve the British–Argentine dispute by Nicholas Ridley when he was Minister of State at the Foreign Office. While this chapter concerns the negotiations of April–May 1982 it is important to remember that Ridley's ideas were reasonable and workable – and that he had no support in parliament. No fewer than eighteen MPs spoke vehemently against the Ridley initiative; some were violently hostile. Among the attackers were Peter Shore, then Labour's spokesman on foreign affairs, Sir Bernard Brain (Conservative), Russell Johnson (Liberal) and Tom McNally (then Labour, later S.D.P.). Mr Shore at that time said that the rights of the islanders 'surely must be of paramount importance'. He seems to have been the first MP to use the word 'paramount' in this connection. On 29 April 1982 Michael Foot urged the Government to consider the idea of U.N. Trusteeship for the islands with 'the greatest care': He recommended acceptance. This would be difficult to reconcile with the Labour Party's fierce insistence eighteen months earlier that no proposal contrary to the paramount wishes of the islanders could be proceeded with: they did not want U.N. Trusteeship.

Few of those who opposed Ridley's plan had much to say during the Commons debates on the Falklands; perhaps some remained silent because they recognised that they had been partly to blame for the crisis which led to the Argentine aggression.

At the end of May 1982, negotiations broke down after seven weeks of tortuous diplomacy. The British Government set out in a public document negotiating positions of both sides. The statement was clear and direct and may be accepted as honest since all documents involved in the negotiations were made public by the United Nations' secretariat. The Secretary General conceded that the position was as set out in the British document, which I have shortened here but have not otherwise altered.

Argentine Aggression
1. Argentina's unlawful use of force in unprovoked aggression in invading the Falkland Islands threatened not only to destroy the democratic way of life freely chosen by the Falkland Islands but also the order on which international order rests. The invasion was also a singular act of bad faith; it took place when Britain and Argentina were engaged in negotiations in accordance with requests from the United Nations.

2. On 1 April the President of the United Nations Security Council had formally appealed to Argentina not to invade the islands. Yet on 2 April Argentina invaded. On 3 April the United Nations Security Council passed its mandatory resolution 502, demanding cessation of hostilities and an immediate

withdrawal of all Argentine forces. The same day Argentina took South Georgia.

The British Response
3. Britain need have done nothing more than rest on the mandatory resolution of the Security Council. Britain's inherent right of self defence under article 51 of the Charter would have justified the Government in adopting a purely military policy for ending the crisis. But in pursuit of a peaceful settlement Britain adopted a policy, frequently explained in parliament, of building up pressure on Argentina ... Diplomatic pressure was built up by the clear statements of condemnation of Argentine aggression which were made by many countries. It was widely recognised that aggression could not be allowed to stand, since otherwise peace and order would be prejudiced in many regions. The members of the European Community, Australia, New Zealand, Canada and Norway joined Britain in imposing economic measures against Argentina, as did the U.S.A. a little later.

Efforts for a Negotiated Settlement
4. Britain dedicated her maximum diplomatic efforts to the search for a negotiated solution ... Efforts for an interim agreement to end the crisis were first undertaken by the U.S. Secretary of State Alexander Haig. His ideas for an interim agreement were discussed repeatedly with Argentina and Britain. The Government expressed willingness to consider Mr Haig's final proposals, although they represented real difficulties. Argentina rejected them. The next

stage was based on the proposals originally advanced by President Bellaunde of Peru and modified by him in consultations with Mr Haig. As the Foreign Secretary told parliament on 7 May Britain was willing to accept the final version of these proposals for an interim agreement. Argentina rejected it.

5. After this the Secretary General of the U.N., Perez de Cueller, conducted negotiations with Britain, through the British ambassador to the U.N., Sir Anthony Parsons, and Argentina through its deputy foreign minister Señor Enrique Ros. In these negotiations Britain made repeated efforts to establish whether Argentina was willing to be sufficiently flexible to make a reasonable interim agreement possible. It became increasingly clear that Argentina was not seeking an agreement but was playing for time in the negotiations ... There was an important meeting of British Ministers, attended by Sir Anthony Parsons and the British Ambassador in Washington, Sir Nicholas Henderson, on 16 May. On the following day Sir Anthony handed to the U.N. Secretary General two documents:

(a) A draft interim agreement between Britain and Argentina which set out the British position in full.

(b) A letter to the Secretary General making clear that the Falkland Islands Dependencies were not covered by draft interim agreements.

6. Sir Anthony Parsons made clear to the Secretary General that the draft agreement was the furthest Britain could go in negotiations. The Secretary

General gave the draft to the Argentine Deputy Foreign Minister. The Argentine reply was received on 19 May; it amounted to a rejection of the British proposals and a hardening of its own position.

Britain's fundamental principles in Negotiation
7. The Government's approach in all negotiations was based on important principles, frequently stated in parliament.

(a) International Law. Argentina's unlawful aggression must end and Resolution 502 must be implemented. Aggression must not be rewarded or small countries everywhere will feel threatened by neighbours with territorial ambitions.

(b) Freedom. The Falkland Islanders are used to enjoying free institutions. The Executive and Legislative Councils were established with their agreement and function with their participation. Britain insisted that any interim administration in the Falklands must involve democratically elected representatives of the islanders ...

(c) Sovereignty. Britain has no doubt of her sovereignty over the islands, having administered them peacefully since 1833. Nevertheless, successive British governments have been willing, without prejudice, to include the question of sovereignty in negotiations with Argentina about the future of the islands ...

8. Britain upheld these principles in the draft agreement presented to the U.N. Secretary General on 17 May.

The agreement provided for complete Argentine withdrawal within fourteen days, thus terminating the aggression and upholding international law. It provided that the Legislative and Executive Councils representing the Falklands Islanders would continue in existence and be consulted by the U.N. interim administrator. It provided explicitly that the outcome of negotiations was not prejudged ...

9. In the Secretary General's negotiations Britain insisted that the Falkland Islands Dependencies should not be covered by an interim agreement ... South Georgia and South Sandwich Islands are geographically distant from the Falkland Islands themselves. They have no settled population. The British title to them does not derive from the Falkland Islands ...

10. Throughout the negotiations Britain has been willing to negotiate on matters where principles were not breached. In particular:

(a) In return for Argentine withdrawal from a zone of 150 miles radius around the Falkland Islands and an undertaking that no forces would return, Britain was willing to withdraw her Task Force from the zone and not return during the interim period. She proposed international verification ... in which the U.N. could have made use of surveillance aircraft from third countries.

(b) Britain was willing that the exclusion zones declared by herself and Argentina and the economic measures be lifted from the moment of ceasefire, although these actions would give more comfort to Argentina than to Britain.

(c) Britain was prepared to accept the appointment of a U.N. Administrator ... Britain was willing to accept one representative from the Argentine population of the islands (thirty people out of 1800) on the Legislative and the Executive councils.

In addition Britain was willing to accept the presence of three Argentine observers on the Islands in the interim period.

(d) Britain was willing to agree to re-establishment of communications, travel, transport, postage etc between the Falklands and Argentina.

(e) Britain was willing to enter into peaceful negotiations under the auspices of the U.N. Secretary General for a peaceful settlement of the dispute and to seek the completion of these negotiations by 31 December 1982.

11. *Argentina's final position on the negotiations*
(a) Argentina insisted that South Georgia and South Sandwich Islands be covered by the interim agreement.

(b) Argentina wanted thirty days for completion of the withdrawal of forces; all forces would return to their normal bases, in the case of British forces, back to England.

(c) Argentina wanted the administration of the Islands to be exclusively the responsibility of the United Nations ...

(d) Argentina wanted free access for her nationals to the Islands, with respect to residence, work and property. Argentina also opposed a provision in the British draft agreement about the U.N. Administrator exercising his powers in conformity with the laws and practices traditionally observed in the islands. It was evident that Argentina hoped to change the nature of Falklands society and its demographic make-up in the interim period.

(e) Argentina proposed a formula about negotiations on the future of the islands which stated that they should be 'initiated' without prejudice to the rights and claims of the two parties. Argentina would not accept an additional phrase stating also that the outcome would not be prejudged ... Argentine leaders made clear that if no definitive agreement was reached by 31 December 1982 Argentina would fill the vacuum.

This was not the complete end of the negotiations. Peru made another attempt to get them started by setting out a list of points, but they were nothing more than topics for a form of agenda of matters to be discussed. Late in May 1982 the U.N. Security Council gave its Secretary General a week in which to find a formula for a cease-fire but he failed. The Irish representative on the Security Council, on the direct instruction from Ireland's prime minister, Charles Haughey, tried to get the Council to pass a resolution calling for a seventy two-hour cease fire. The Japanese and the Brazilians also made ill-considered suggestions which proved abortive.

Then followed a motion by Panama and Spain calling for a ceasefire. Since this would have left the Argentinians in possession of Port Stanley and provided an opportunity for reinforcement and resupply, Britain vetoed the motion. The United States also voted against the motion but its U.N. ambassador, Jeane Kirkpatrick, announced moments later that on behalf of her government she really should have abstained. She had just received an instruction from Mr Haig to do so. This peculiar performance was enacted while Mrs Thatcher and President Reagan were in Paris, demonstrating the warmth and closeness of the British–American relationship. For a time the incident jeopardised that relationship and Senator Charles Percy called Mrs Kirkpatrick an 'unguided missile'. Mrs Kirkpatrick, who wrote her PhD dissertation at Columbia University on Argentina during the Peron years, considers herself the Administration's premier expert on Latin America. She spoke against the U.S. providing the British with military intelligence and equipment; she met in New York, in June 1982, Argentine Air Force Brigadier Joset Miret, a political-military strategist on the Argentine government to discuss U.N. peace initiatives; she conferred with the Deputy Argentine Foreign Minister Enrique Ros, in the apartment of one of her own assistants. And all this without the prior knowledge of her superior, Mr Haig.

After the breakdown of negotiations Mrs Thatcher withdrew the British offers, although several prominent Opposition members, including Michael Foot, David Owen and David Steel, urged her to let

192

them 'lie on the table'. Mrs Thatcher's attitude was that a completely different set of circumstances prevailed. Argentina had rejected the British proposals. Logically, Britain could not in any way bring Argentina into a form of administration of the islands. There was a limit, she said, to which Britain could go. Indeed, the British negotiators had already gone too far and had offered the Argentine government the thin end of a wedge with which to prize out the British. The Argentinians, in possession of the islands and blinded by nationalist passion, declined to accept it. At that point the war which need not have happened became 'the war that had to be'.

APPENDIX

Falkland Facts

After two sightings in 1592 and 1594, both by British navigators, the first landing in the islands was made by Captain Strong of H.M.S. *Welfare*, who named them after Viscount Falkland.

The first settlement was made by the French, at Port Louis, East Falkland, in 1764. Two years later a British settlement of about 400 people was established. In 1767 the French sold Port Louis to Spain, an act which may have started the first Falkland crisis. In 1770, when Argentina was still a dominion of the Kingdom of Spain, the Governor of Buenos Aires, Buccarelli, sent a squadron of five Spanish ships to seize West Falkland.

In Port Stanley the Spanish found the frigates H.M.S. *Favourite* and *Swift*, supported by a shore battery in the Port Stanley fort, Egremont. No fighting occurred and after three weeks of negotiation the British ships withdrew in the face of overwhelming opposition.

What happened then was similar to what took place in 1982. When the news of the outrage reached London the Government and Opposition were equally enraged and the garrison was criticised as feeble and cowardly. The government negotiated with Madrid and at the same time fitted out a strong

195

task force. Diplomatic pressure was successful and in January 1771 the King of Spain announced that Governor Buccarelli had exceeded his authority and that the territory would be returned to Britain, which was duly done.

Dr Samuel Johnson wrote at the time that it was not worthwhile going to war for a place as useless as the Falklands. 'They were a harsh, inhospitable and costly addition to the Crown ... a bleak and gloomy solitude, stormy in winter and barren in summer ...'

The British allowed the Spanish to settle in the Falklands in 1774 but the Spaniards finally relinquished any claim to the islands in 1810. By 1811 the only occupants were at the British settlement on the west island and a British sealing and whaling base on the east island.

For the next twenty years there was no real authority on the islands. In 1829 an enterprising German with a French name, Vernet, acquired the title to much land and had himself appointed governor by the new Argentine government in Buenos Aires. But when Vernet seized three American whalers, an American warship threw him out of the Falklands and burned his settlement. A nominal Argentine settlement existed between 1829 and 1833 but it was not continuous; the majority of the approximately one hundred people were Indians, sent there as slaves, and none of the overseers were of Argentine origin.

Reports of lawlessness reached London and H.M.S. *Challenger* was sent to the Falklands; the ship's first officer, Lieutenant Smith, was installed as governor in 1833. More Britons arrived as settlers and British governorship was continuous until May 1982.

Various British companies and families bought land and by 1982 seventy per cent of the land was owned by companies registered in the UK. The best-known landlord is the Falklands Islands Company, founded by Royal Charter in 1851 and now owned by the Coalite Group from Derby. Coalite employed half the island's population before the Argentinian invasion and owned forty per cent of the sheep.

Another thirty per cent is owned by seven small private companies in Britain and Jersey. James Lovegrove Waldron Ltd with thirty-seven British shareholders owns the 170,000 acres of Port Howard, with 38,000 sheep. The Cameron family, owners of Port San Carlos Ltd, have 91,000 acres and 31,000 sheep. Holmestead, Blake and Company has 140,000 acres at Hill Cove in West Falkland and Dean Brothers own most of Pebble Island, in the form of a 36,000 acre sheep farm.

The Argentine government bases its claim to the islands on two grounds – proximity and early settlement. The Falklands at their nearest point to South America are 300 miles from the entrance to the Straits of Magellan. On the basis of proximity the sovereignty of scores of places would be questionable. Cuba is ninety miles west of Key West in Florida; Taiwan lies one hundred miles off the Chinese mainland; Rhodes, inhabited by Greeks, lies fifteen miles from Turkey. And the Channel Islands would be French rather than British.

If the four-year non-continuous settlement of the Islas Malvinas (1829–1833) constitutes a claim for sovereignty, Louisiana and Quebec should be French, the state of Delaware should belong to Sweden, while Texas, New Mexico, Arizona and southern California could be Mexican. The Russians could claim all of northern California and the Northeast United States would revert to British rule, with Canada managing the region for the British.

Some Argentinians claim the Malvinas for what their Nobel Peace Prize Winner Adolofo Esquivel calls 'historic, legal and geographical reasons'. Esquivel argues that the islands 'are held [by Britain] in a colonial relationship'. But the only people who could be entitled to argue such an allegation are a colonised people – and the Falkland Islanders do not perceive such a relationship. The tiny British garrison on the islands was present protectively and by request and not coercively by imposition. Many peoples have demanded freedom from colonial rule but the Falkland Islanders have never sought 'freedom' because it was never denied them, until the Argentinian invasion of 1982. Then, for the first time, many of them knew what it was like to be locked up as captives.

On the grounds of capital expended the Falklands are British. This expenditure has never been adequate but the Overseas Development Administration has spent £1m a year for projects and salaries and has provided forty officials vital to the running of the islands. Before the invasion crisis the Falklands Islands Company and the Overseas Development Administration, with some paternalistic help from the Falklands Islands Office in London, were planning to continue their low-key development projects. They could not stop the slow emigration but with land made available to smallholders the drift could be stopped and even reversed, on the principle that small farmers have greater incentive than paid labourers or the big, distant company boards.

On the day of Argentina's invasion the Governor was to hand over the deeds of six small farms of about 6,000 acres each to young men who wanted to break away from 'the company' and farm on their own account.

The islanders themselves perpetuated British rule by passing the Falklands Islands Aliens Ordinance which prevents aliens, other than 'licensed aliens', from owning or holding property in the Falklands Islands. It also gives the governor power to expel anybody judged by him and the Council to be an undesirable alien. It is not possible, under the Ordinance, for an islander to sell property to a wealthy Argentinian or other South American. While the Ordinance might be questionable – on the grounds that it is a racist immigration policy – it nevertheless emphasises the islanders' desire for independence from other peoples and their dependence on British links. Lord Shackleton in his report emphasised this feeling of dependence. 'Their sense of identity reflects mainly their strong awareness of their British origins and they do not yet seem to have evolved a distinctive local culture which could further their self confidence.'

The *Economist* sent a team to report on the Falklands economy in 1980. It made some interesting statements, including this one: 'Although versatile, the population tends to show a marked degree of dependence on government, on employers and on the United Kingdom ...'

It is only fair to say that many Falkland Islanders, though British by blood and passport, had no great love for Britain before the Argentine take-over. This was understandable because one British government after another had done little to help the islands become developed, despite promises to do so. The Falklanders only discovered how British they were when they awoke to the terrible fear that they might lose their Britishness. At that point they became patriotic. This is not meant to be a cynical comment, and its truth in no way supports the Argentinian claim to sovereignty.

If the Falkland Islanders themselves wanted to change from British to Argentine nationality they would have a right to do so; they could 'go independent' but they are dependent economically on ties to some larger political entity. Those ties lie with Britain despite links of convenience with Uruguay and to a lesser extent, Argentina. International law and a vast mass of treaties and documents including the United Nations Charter, condemn military aggression and the subjugation of a populace by force of arms. Thus, the Falkland islanders have the right to resist occupation and to seek help from their homeland.

I am advised by several professors of international law that Argentina has no claim in law on the Falklands. Equally it has no claim in history or geography – and none in logic. 'Prescription' – the term for very long unbroken occupation of territory – gives Britain the legal advantage.

* Samuel Johnson's 1771 assertion that the Falklands were not worth fighting for was echoed by many people in 1982, though he was speaking of real estate rather than principle. He made two other observations at the same time.

* 'Who does not know that a foreign war has often put a stop to civil discords? It withdraws the attention of the public from domestic grievances and affords opportunities of dismissing the turbulent and restless to distant employment.' In 1982 the Galtieri-Anaya-Dozo Junta had much civil discord and domestic discord which they wanted to divert.

* 'We have gained political strength by the increase in our reputation,' said Johnson. 'We have gained real strength by the reparation [restoration] of our Navy.' As in 1771, so in 1982.

ROLL OF HONOUR

'We are the Pilgrims, Master:
We shall go always a little further:
It may be beyond that last blue mountain barr'd
   with snow,
Across that angry or that glimmering Sea.'
         (From the S.A.S. Memorial to their dead.
         22 S.A.S., Bradbury Lines Camp,
         Hereford)

This is the list of those who died in the Falklands War; some are 'presumed dead' only because their bodies were not recovered. A few omissions are probable and there may be some mistakes in spelling. This is because the Ministry of Defence announced that it was not keeping a continuing and consolidated list of casualties and because it did not respond to my specific inquiries.

April 23
Petty Officer (Aircrewman) Kevin Casey,
Portland, killed in helicopter accident,
H.M.S. *Hermes*.

May 4
Lt. Nicholas Taylor, 33, Yeovilton, Fleet Air Arm
   Sea Harrier pilot.

H.M.S. *Sheffield*

Lt.-Cdr. John Woodhead, 36.

Lt.-Cdr. David Balfour, 37, Hindhead.

Sub-Lt. Richard Emly, 36, Havant.

Master at Arms Brian Welsh, 34, Gateshead.

P.O. David Briggs, 25, Lee-on-Solent.

P.O. Robert Fagan, 34, Stubbington.

A/Chief Weapons Eng. Mech. Michael Till, 35, Stubbington.

Weapons Elec. Artificer One Kevin Sullivan, 35, Porchester.

Weapons Eng. Mech. Two Barry Wallis, 26, Porchester.

Cook Neil Goodall, 20, Enfield.

Weapons Elec. Artificer One Anthony Eggington, 35, Purbrock.

Cook Andrew Swallow, 18, Bembridge.

Leading Cook Tony Marshall, 31, Gosport.

P.O. Weapons Eng. Mech. (Radio) Anthony Norman, 25, Gosport.

Leading Marine Eng. Mech. Allan Knowles, 31, Gosport.

Cook David Osborne, 22, Portsmouth.

Leading Cook Adrian Wellstead, 26, Portsmouth.

Lai Chi Keung, 31, Hong Kong.

Catering Assistant Darryl Cope, 21, Stourport-on-Severn.

Cook Kevin Williams, 20, Gosport.

May 6

Lt.-Cdr. John Eyton-Jones, 39, Ilchester. Sea Harrier pilot.

Lt. William Curtis, 35, Crewkerne, Sea Harrier pilot.

May 19–20

S.A.S. men killed in helicopter operations (parent unit given):

W.O.2 L. Gallagher, Royal Engineers.

W.O.2 M. Atkinson, Coldstream Guards.

Staff Sgt. P. O'Connor, Irish Guards.

Sgt. P. Currass, Royal Army Medical Corps.

Sgt. S. Davidson, Parachute Regiment.

Sgt. J. Arthy, Welsh Guards.

Cpl. P. Bunker, Royal Army Ordnance Corps.

Cpl. W. Begley, Royal Corps of Transport.

Cpl. W. Hatton, Parachute Regiment.

Cpl. P. Jones, Welsh Guards.

Cpl. J. Newton, Royal Army Mech. & Elec. Engineers.

Cpl. M. McHugh, Royal Signals.

Cpl. S. Sykes, Royal Signals.

Cpl. E. Walpole, Royal Green Jackets.

Cpl. M. Burns, Royal Signals.

Cpl. D. MacCormack, Royal Signals.

L/Cpl. P. Lightfoot, Royal Signals.

Rifleman R. Armstrong, Royal Green Jackets.

Helicopter crew:

Flight-Lt. Garth Hawkins RAF.

Cpl. Michael Love, Royal Marines.

May 21

San Carlos operations:

H.M.S. *Ardent*

Able Seaman (Sonar) Derek Armstrong, 22, Prudhoe, Northumbria.

Lt.-Cdr. Richard Banfield, 30, Liskeard.

Able Seaman (Sonar) Andrew Barr, 20, Bridgwater.

P.O. Air Eng. (Mech.) Peter Brouard, 31, Crewkerne.

Cook Richard Dunkerley, 23, Windsor.

Acting Leading Cook Michael Foot, 24, Warren Park, Havant.

Marine Eng. Mech. Stephen Ford, 18, Poole.

Act. Steward Shaun Hanson, 20, Ecclesfield, Sheffield.

Able Seaman Sean Hayward, 18, Barrow-in-Furness.

Able Seaman Stephen Heyes, 22, St Budeaux, Devonport.

Weapons Eng. Mech. Simon Lawson, 21, Whitley Bay, Northumberland.

Marine Eng. Mech. Alistair Leighton, 19, Margate.

Air Eng. Mech. Allan McAuley, 36, Yeovilton.

Act. Leading Seaman Michael Mullen, 24, Roby, Liverpool.

Lt. Brian Murphy, 30, Yeovil.

Leading Physical Training Instructor Gary Nelson, 25, Saltash.

Cook John Roberts, 26, Gwynedd, North Wales.

Lt.-Cdr. John Sephton, 35, Preston, Dorset.

Act. Leading Marine Eng. Mech. Stephen White, 21, Washington, Tyne & Wear.

Acting P.O. Weapons Eng. Mech. Andrew Palmer, 26, Truro.

Acting Leading Marine Eng. Mech. Garry Whitford, 23, Blackburn.

Marine Eng. Mech. Gilbert Williams, 21, Kidlington, Oxfordshire.

Able Seaman Ian Boldy, 20, Derby.
Seaman Matthew Stuart, 18, Tewkesbury.

Gazelle helicopters: Royal Marines
Lt. Kenneth Francis, 29, Lyndhurst.
Sgt. Andrew Evans, 33, Landrake, Cornwall.
L/Cpl. Brett Giffen, 24, Plympton, Plymouth.

May 22
H.M.S. *Antelope*
Steward M. R. Stephens, 18, Mansfield.
Staff Sgt. James Prescott, Royal Engineers, 37,
    Rochester.

May 24
Sea Harrier, H.M.S. *Hermes*
Lt.-Cdr. G. W. J. Batt, 37, Yeovil.

May 25
H.M.S. *Coventry*
Marine Eng. Mech. Frank Armes, 21, Norwich.
Acting Chief Weapons Eng. Artificer John Cadby,
    34, Emsworth.
Marine Eng. Artificer Paul Callus, 24, Emsworth.
Acting P.O. Catering Accountant Stephen Dawson,
    23, Scunthorpe.
Acting Weapons Eng. Mech. (Radio) John
    Dobson, 20, Exeter.
P.O. (Sonar) Michael Fowlet, 36, Southsea.
Weapons Eng. Mech. (Ordnance) Ian Hall, 22,
    Cowley.
Lt. Rodney Heath RN, 34, Gosport.
Acting Weapons Eng. Mech. David Ozbirn, 33,
    Bishops Waltham.

Lt.-Cdr. Glen Robinson-Moltke, 37, Petersfield.
Leading Radio Operator Bernard Still, 26, C.
  Laoise, Eire.
Marine Eng. Artificer Geoffrey Stockwell, 23,
  Herne Bay.
Acting Weapons Eng. Artificer David Strickland,
  29, Harrow.
Able Seaman (Electronic Warfare) Adrian
  Sunderland, 18, Sherborne.
Marine Eng. Mech. Stephen Tonkin, 20,
  Sheffield.
Acting Cook Ian Turnbull, 17, Hartlepool.
Acting Weapons Eng. Artificer Philip White, 26,
  Pangbourne.
Weapons Eng. Artificer/Apprentice Ian Williams,
  21, South Wirral.
Kyo Ben Kwo, Shaukiwan, Hong Kong.

Atlantic Conveyor
Captain Ian North, 57, Doncaster.
Bosun John Dobson, 58, Devon.
Frank Foulkes, 48, Kirkham, Lancs.
James Hughes, 48, Gosport.
Ernest Vickers, 58, Middlesborough.
David Hawkins, 42, Newquay.
Air Eng. Mech. (Radio) One A.U. Anslow, 20,
  Tettenhall.
Chief P.O. Writer E. Flanagan, 35, Gillingham.
Leading Air Eng. Mech. Elec. D. Pryce, 26,
  Gosport.
Chief Radio Officer R. Hoole, 37, Matlock.
Ng Po, Hong Kong.
Chan Chi Shing, Hong Kong.

San Carlos Air Attack:

Royal Marines
Sgt. A. Enefer, 34, Plympton, Plymouth.
L/Cpl. P. McKay, 19, Macduff, Banffshire.
Marine C. Davison, 21, Killingsworth, Newcastle-upon-Tyne.
Marine S. McAndrews, 22 Wythenshawe, Manchester.
Cpl. K. Evans, 36, Waterlooville, Hampshire.
Lieut. Richard Nunn, 28, helicopter pilot, Looe.

May 28
Recapture of Goose Green:
2nd Battalion The Parachute Regiment
Lt.-Col. Herbert Jones, 42, Fleet, Hampshire.
Lt. James Barry, 29, St. Albans.
L/Cpl. Gary Bingley, 24, Aldershot.
Cpl. Anthony Cork, 21, Aldershot.
Captain Christopher Dent, 34, Farnborough.
Pte Stephen Dixon, 18, Basildon.
Pte Mark Fletcher, 21, Stockport.
Cpl. David Hardman, 22, Hamilton, Scotland.
Pte Mark Holman-Smith, 19, Bodmin.
Pte Stephen Illingsworth, 20, Doncaster.
Pte Thomas Mechan, 25, Glasgow.
Cpl. Stephen Prior, 27, Brighton.
L/Cpl. Nigel Smith, 21, Aldershot.
Cpl. Paul Sullivan, 27, Aldershot.
Captain David Wood, 29, Gillingham.

59 Independent Commando Squadron Royal Engineers
Cpl. Michael Melia, 30, Plymouth.
Sapper Pradeep Kumar Gandhi, 24, Wembley.

June 8

Gazelle helicopter crash, East Falkland:
Royal Signals
Major Mike Forge, 40, Rochester.
Staff Sgt. Joe Baker, 36, Rothwell,
  Northamptonshire.

Army Air Corps
Staff Sgt. C. Griffin, 32, Aldershot.
L/Cpl. Simon Cockton, 22, Camberley.

Royal Marines
Acting Sgt. I. Hunt, 28, Poole.

June 10

S.A.S. Regiment
Captain Gavin Hamilton, 29, The Green Howards,
  Hereford.

June 8

Air Attack on Bluff Cove:
Royal Fleet Auxiliary Sir Galahad
Royal Army Medical Corps
Major Roger Nutbeem, 40, Aldershot.

Welsh Guards
L/Cpl. Barry Bullers, 26, Walsall.
L/Cpl. Anthony Burke, 23, Pirbright.
L/Sgt. James Carlyle, 26, Ruthin.
Guardsman Ian Dale, 19, Pontypridd.
Guardsman Michael Dunphy, 23, Llechryd, Clwyd.

Guardsman Peter Edwards, 19, Denbigh.
Sgt. Clifford Elley, 29, Pirbright.
Guardsman Mark Gibby, 22, Wattstown, Rhondda.
Guardsman Glenn Grace, 20, Newport.
Guardsman Paul Green, 21, Rhyl.
Guardsman Gareth Griffiths, 31, Pirbright.
Guardsman Denis Hughes, 22, Wrexham.
Guardsman Gareth Hughes, 22, Llanfairfechan,
    Gwynedd.
Guardsman Brian Jasper, 26, Pirbright.
Guardsman Anthony Keeble, 19, Pontyclun,
    Glamorgan.
L/Sgt. Kevin Keoghane, 30, Pirbright.
Guardsman Michael Marks, 17, Stamford-le-Hope,
    Essex.
Guardsman Christopher Mordecai, 18, Maesteg,
    Glamorgan.
L/Cpl. Stephen Newbury, 24, Pirbright.
Guardsman Gareth Nicholson, 19, Woking.
Guardsman Colin Parsons, 18, Cardiff.
Guardsman Eirwyn Phillips, 20, Carmarthen.
Guardsman Gareth Poole, 20, Pontypridd.
Guardsman Nigel Rowberry, 20, Cardiff.
L/Cpl. Phillip Sweet, 22, Pirbright.
Guardsman Glyn Thomas, 20, Cardiff.
L/Cpl. Nicholas Thomas, 25, Llanelli.
Guardsman Raymond Thomas, 28, Barry.
Guardsman Andrew Walker, 20, York.
L/Cpl. Christopher Ward, 22, Feltham, Middlesex.
Guardsman James Weaver, 20, Port Talbot.
Sgt. Malcolm Wigley, 31, Woking.
Guardsman David Williams, 21, Holyhead.

16 Field Ambulance
L/Cpl. Ian Farrell, 24, Everton.
Pte. Kenneth Preston, 21, St Helens.

Army Catering Corps
Pte. R. W. Middlewick, 21, Brighton.
Pte. Michael Jones, Carmarthen.

9 Para Squadron Royal Engineers
Cpl. Andrew McIlvenny, 28, Rainham, Kent.
Sapper Wayne Tabard, 19, Derby.

Royal Electrical & Mechanical Engineers
Craftsman Mark Rollins, 25, Birmingham.
L/Cpl. Anthony Streatfield, 22, Woking.

R.F.A. Sir Galahad crew
Third Eng. Officer Christopher Hailwood, 26,
  Farnborough.
Second Eng. Officer Paul Henry, 34, Berwick-on-
  Tweed.
Electrical Fitter Leung Chau Dis, 61, Hong Kong.
Third Eng. Officer Andrew Morris, 25, Poole.
Butcher Sung Yuk Fai Dis, 51, Hong Kong.

R.F.A. Sir Tristram crew
Bosun Yuk Sik Chee, 60, Hong Kong.
Sailor Yung Shui Kam, 43, Hong Kong.

Royal Marines Landing Craft
Marine Robert Griffin, 22, Sheffield.
Colour Sgt. Brian Johnston, 34, Exmouth.
Sgt. Ronal Rotheram, 34, Cerne Abbas, Dorset.

Marine Anthony Rundle, 26, Cheadle.

Royal Navy
Marine Eng. Artificer Alexander James, 32, Bishops
   Waltham.
Acting Leading Marine Eng. Mech. David Miller,
   22, Pagham.

June 12
H.M.S. *Glamorgan*
P.O. Air Eng. Mech. Michael Adcock, 34,
   Fortuneswell, Dorset.
Cook Brian Easton, 24, Portsmouth.
Acting Chief Air Eng. Mech. David Lee, 35, Leeds.
Air Eng. Artificier Mech. Two Kelvin McCullum,
   25, Portland.
Cook Brian Malcolm, 22, Gosport.
Leading Cook Mark Sambles, 29, Portsmouth.
Leading Cook Anthony Sillence, 26, Doncaster.
Steward John Stroud, 20, Gosport.
Lieut. David Tinker, 25, Rochester.
P.O. Aircrewman Colin Vickers, 33, Wyke Regis.
Air Eng. Mech. One Mark Henderson, 20, Glasgow.
Air Eng. Mech. (Radio) One Brian Hinge, 24, Bristol.
Marine Eng. Mech. Two Terence Perkins, 19,
   Cardiff.

June 11–14
Retaking of Port Stanley 11–14 June:

Royal Marines
Sgt. Robert Leeming, 32, Arbroath.
Cpl. Andrew Uren, 23, Lapford, Devon.

Cpl. Peter Fitton, 25, Bilston.
Marine Keith Phillips, 19, Dartford.
Cpl. Jeremy Smith, 23, Torquay.
Cpl. Laurence Watts, 27, Watford.
Marine Gordon Macpherson, 20, Oban.
Marine Michael Nowak, 23, Derby.
Cpl. Ian Spencer, 26, Arbroath.

3rd Battalion The Parachute Regiment
Pte. Mark Dodsworth, 24, Tidworth.
Sgt. Ian McKay, 29, Aldershot.
Cpl. Stewart McLaughlin, 27, Tidworth.
Cpl. Keith McCarthy, 27, Aldershot.
L/Cpl. David Scott, 24, Tidworth.
L/Cpl. Christopher Lovett, 24, Tidworth.
L/Cpl. James Murdoch, 25, Renfrew.
Pte. Gerald Bull, 18, Brixworth, Northamptonshire.
Pte. Jonathan Crow, 21, Tonbridge.
Pte. Jason Burt, 17, Walthamstow.
Pte. Anthony Greenwood, 22, Manchester.
Pte. Neil Grose, 18, Gosport.
Pte. Peter Hedicker, 22, Aldershot.
Pte. Timothy Jenkins, 19, Ross-on-Wye.
Pte. Ian Scrivens, 17, Yeovil.
Pte. Stewart Laing, 20, Lanchester.
Pte. Philip West, 19, Newcastle-upon-Tyne.
Pte. Craig Jones, 20, Greens Norton,
    Northamptonshire.
Cpl. Scot Wilson, 25, 9th Para Squadron R.E.,
    attached 3 Para.
Sapper Christopher Jones, 29, 59 Independent
    Commando Squadron R.E. attached to Royal
    Marines, Cindersford, Glos.

Craftsman Alexander Shaw, 25, R.E.M.E., attached
3 Para, Tidworth.

2nd Battalion The Scots Guards
Guardsman David Malcolmson, 20, Irvine.
Guardsman Archibald Stirling, 21, Glasgow.
Guardsman James Reynolds, 19, Renfrew.
Guardsman Derek Denholm, 24, Edinburgh.
Guardsman John Simeon, 36, Chelsea.
Guardsman Ronald Tanbini, 25, Dundee.
L/Sgt. Clark Mitchell, 26, Edinburgh.
W.O. 2 Daniel Wight, 37, Edinburgh.

2nd Battalion The Parachute Regiment
Pte. David Parr, 19, Lowestoft.
Pte. Francis Slough, 19, Reading.
Colour Sgt. Gordon Finlay, 32, Aldershot.

Welsh Guards
L/Cpl. Christopher Thomas, 22, Poole.

9 Para Squadron Royal Engineers
L/Cpl. John Pashley, 22, Eckington, Derbyshire.

Died of Wounds
Marine Paul Callan, 21, Great Sutton, South Wirral.
Cpl. Stephen Hope, 27, 3rd Bn Parachute Regt,
Manchester.
Pte. Richard Absolon, 19, 3rd Bn Parachute Regt,
Weybridge.